BIG
BOOK
OF FUN

Creative Learning Activities for Home and School, Ages 4–12

Carolyn Buhai Haas

Illustrated by Jane Bennett Phillips

CHICAGO REVIEW PRESS

Other Books Coauthored by Carolyn B. Haas
I Saw a Purple Cow
A Pumpkin in a Pear Tree
Children Are Children Are Children
Backyard Vacation
Purple Cow to the Rescue!
Look At Me

LC No. 87-20325

Printed in the United States of America
Second edition

ISBN 1-55652-020-4
Published by CHICAGO REVIEW PRESS INCORPORATED, 814 N. Franklin, Chicago IL 60610

To my granddaughter, Lisa Ann Haas
and her grandfather, Bob Haas
and our children
Andy and Susan, Mari and Jim,
Betsy and Arthur, Tom, and Karen

ACKNOWLEDGMENTS

I owe a special debt of gratitude to Betty Weinberger and Ann Cole, who have allowed me to use some of the material that we developed as the PAR team.

I am also grateful to the many others who have helped make this book possible: Jane Phillips and Carol Mansfield for their helpful suggestions and delightful artwork; Doris Welter, Irene Feltes and Paula Levy, who served as typists, critics and general assistants; Christine Sutton, Ellen Gundersen and Beth Pritchard who patiently set and re-set the type; Elizabeth Cater, Larry Rood, Marc Barz and Fred Chaimson for their encouragement and support; Sandra Barz, Ilse Jacobson, Faith Bushnell, Elizabeth Heller, Sheila Handler, Joan Loeb, Jane Shadlen, Dixie Trout and countless other writers, friends and children, who contributed ideas, tested recipes and projects, and helped get this BIG BOOK OF FUN together.

While doing the research and writing, I found the following publications to be especially helpful: *Tot-Line, Practical Parenting* and *Parenting* newsletters; *Instructor, Early Years, Learning, Teacher, Family Circle, Sunset* and *Parents* magazines.

A list of other valuable books and resources can be found at the end of the book.

CONTENTS

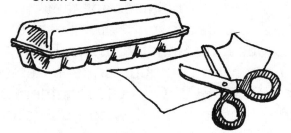

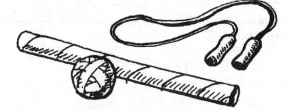

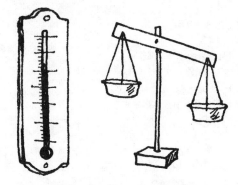

COOKING FUN

HOLIDAY RECIPES

INTRODUCTION

Welcome to THE BIG BOOK OF FUN, a storehouse bursting with creative learning activities to use at home or in the classroom. The easy-to-use format and the abundance of appealing illustrations will captivate children from pre-school through grade 6.

Included in the child-tested, age-sequenced activities are arts and crafts projects; ideas for making toys and games; science and nature projects; songs, poems and fingerplays; indoor and outdoor games; reading and math readiness activities; easy, nutritious cooking ideas; holiday and party fun . . . and much, much more . . . to help children think, create and be motivated to learn through play.

Children will be intrigued with the wide range of creative, success-oriented projects that require only a few inexpensive ''junk'' materials such as egg cartons, boxes and bags, along with a few basic supplies like scissors, crayons and glue.

Parents will welcome the many suggestions for family fun, and for keeping kids productively occupied during those difficult times when a child is tired, sick in bed or has been cooped up too long indoors.

Teachers will recognize the underlying learning value and skill reinforcement inherent in each of the projects, as well as the opportunity to open up communications between school and home.

Grandparents, babysitters . . . in fact, everyone who works with children will appreciate the convenience of having a cornucopia of imaginative activities right at their fingertips.

All of the projects in THE BIG BOOK OF FUN have been designed to be open-ended and flexible, enabling them to be expanded, simplified and adapted to various age levels, needs and occasions. They can be enjoyed by just one child alone, a small group, or an entire classroom. And above all, the ideas are meant to be suggestions that will serve as springboards to further creativity and learning.

So start looking through the pages, plunge in and enjoy. You're sure to find dozens of new (and some old, tried and true) activities to make life with and for children more fun!

HANDY TO SAVE

CONTAINERS

- oatmeal, cornmeal and grits cartons
- margarine tubs
- berry baskets
- egg cartons
- boxes and cans of all sizes
- cardboard, styrofoam grocery trays
- cardboard tubes from toilet tissue, paper towels and hangers

ODDS AND ENDS

- buttons
- spools
- jar lids
- cereal bits
- beans rice
- macaroni
- popsicle sticks
- bottle caps
- keys, corks
- stamps
- envelopes
- straws
- toothpicks
- styrofoam
- paper plates AND cups
- feathers, rocks

SCRAPS OF...
- paper
- ribbon
- yarn
- string
- wrapping paper

DRESS UP CLOTHES
- shoes
- ties & belts
- old dresses, skirts
- old hats
- jewelry
- shawls
- glasses

THINGS FOR PUPPETS
- mittens
- gloves
- socks
- nylons
- cloth scraps

DON'T FORGET
- newspapers
- magazines
- paper bags of all sizes
- shirt cardboards

HANDY TO BUY

- Crayons
- Pencils, chalk
- Scissors
- Paste or glue
- Masking or transparent tape
- Watercolor or tempera paint and brushes
- Felt tip markers
- Food coloring
- Construction paper
- Crepe paper

NOTE: BUY ONLY THE ESSENTIALS! Try to save as many usable items as you can. DON'T THROW IT AWAY – SAVE IT!

HELPFUL HINTS

1. A few minutes of PRE-PLANNING can lead to hours of constructive play, with or without supervision.

2. It is not the COMPLETED PRODUCT that is the most important, but rather the PROCESS OF LEARNING through DOING.

3. Children love to be PRAISED for a job well done. They also enjoy seeing their work displayed on wall or refrigerator.

PASTE RECIPES

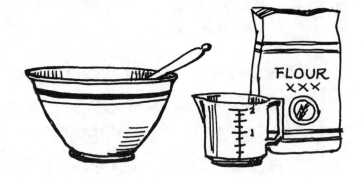

EASY PASTE
You Need:
- ½ cup water
- 1 cup flour

You Do:
1. Just mix the flour and water together in a bowl using a spoon or your hand.

PASTE #2
You Need:
- 1 cup sugar
- 1 cup flour
- 1 teaspoon alum (a preservative)
- 4 cups boiling water
- a few drops of oil of cloves to give the paste a pleasant smell.

You Do:
1. Mix together the sugar, flour and alum, and gradually add the water.
2. Continue cooking over medium heat, stirring until the mixture thickens.
3. Add the oil of cloves and let cool.
4. Store in a covered jar.

WHEAT PASTE
You Need:
- 1½ cups of boiling water
- 2 teaspoons of wheat flour
- ½ teaspoon salt

You Do:
Mix all of the ingredients together and store in a covered jar.

FINGER PAINT RECIPES

FINGER PAINT
You Need:
- paste or liquid starch
- 1 or 2 spoonfuls of soap flakes (or powdered detergent)
- a few drops of food coloring or powdered paint

You Do:
1. Mix the paste, soap flakes and food coloring together in a bowl.
2. Whip with an egg beater until fluffy.
3. Fill several small containers or a muffin tin with paste or liquid laundry starch.
4. Then mix in a few drops of food coloring or powdered tempera paint into each one. (If you start with the primary colors: red, yellow and blue, you can mix them to make other colors.) For texture, stir in some sand, salt or coffee grounds.
5. Place some shiny paper (shelf paper works well) on your table, or paint directly on a vinyl-topped one.
6. Using a wet sponge, dampen the paper, or hold it under a faucet for a few minutes.
7. Put down a dab of paint on top of the paper and begin your finger painting.
8. Use your whole hand, your palm, the side of your hand and your fingers to make swirls, whirls, curves, curvy and straight lines. Add more paint if you wish (not too many colors or your picture will turn muddy) and keep making designs until you get tired.
9. Spread your paper out to dry; if it is too crinkly, put it between some newspaper and iron over it.
10. An old shirt for a smock, newspapers or plastic on the floor and a sponge for cleaning up, will save the day!

Here are some more ways to make finger paint. Use the one that sounds best to you, or try all of them to find which is the most fun.

FINGER PAINT #2
You Need:

- 1 cup cornstarch
- 2 cups of cold water
- 2 envelopes of unflavored gelatin
- 1 cup of soap flakes (or powdered detergent)

You Do:
1. Dissolve the cornstarch in 1½ cups of cold water.
2. Soak the gelatin in the remaining cold water and add to the cornstarch.
3. Cook over medium heat until thick and glossy, stirring occasionally.
4. Blend in the soapflakes and stir well.
5. Add powdered paint or food coloring and store in jars or containers with lids.

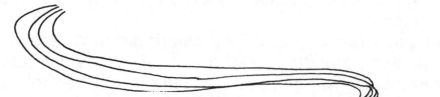

#3 EASY CORNSTARCH FINGERPAINT
You Need:

- 3 tablespoons sugar
- ½ cup cornstarch
- 2 cups cold water
- powdered or tempera paint or food coloring

You Do:
1. Mix sugar, cornstarch and water together and cook over low heat until thick, stirring constantly.
2. Cool and pour into a muffin tin adding a different color to each one.

#4 ANOTHER WAY
You Need:

- ½ cup liquid laundry starch
- 3 cups water
- ¼ cup soap flakes (or powdered detergent)
- ¼ cup talcum powder
- food coloring or tempera paint

You Do:
1. Dissolve the soap flakes in water; then mix in the starch. Cook until the mixture boils and gets clear, stirring constantly.
2. Remove from the stove and add the soap flakes and talcum powder.
3. Beat with an egg beater until smooth and foamy.
4. Store in a covered container in the refrigerator.

TASTY PAINT

Karo syrup, mixed with a tiny bit of tempera powder paint, makes a sticky but tasty finger paint. Pudding also provides licking good finger paint fun. Using warm finger paint will feel good on a cold or rainy day.

FINGERPAINT FUN

PAINTING BAGS

Place a few spoonfuls of colorful finger paint inside a large plastic bag. Lock it tightly (you could also secure with cloth tape for double protection). Place the bag down on a flat surface, then start painting. To erase your design, just rub your hand over the bag. Take along this handy painting bag when you're going on a trip, or waiting to see your doctor or dentist.

FINGERPAINT AND TISSUEPAPER SHAPES
1. Put a glob of paint or some liquid starch in the middle of a dampened sheet of shiny paper.
2. Sprinkle tempera paint on top, blend together and spread it out over the paper.
3. Make a design with your fingers, and while still wet, press down torn or cut-out tissue paper shapes in any kind of a pattern you wish. If you **overlap** any of the shapes, you should probably add a little more fingerpaint between them.
4. Brush over the top of your design with white glue thinned with water.

CRAYON AND FINGERPAINT PRINTS
1. Cover your paper with different colors of crayons, pressing hard.
2. Then brush over the crayoned surface with fingerpaint of a **dark** color.
3. Make a design with your fingers.
4. Cover the painting with another sheet of paper, smooth over it with your hands, and lift it up. You'll have a **print** of your picture!

PLAY DOUGH RECIPES

YOU NEED:

- 1 Cup flour
- ⅓ Cup salt
- ⅓ to ½ Cup water
- a few drops of liquid detergent or vegetable oil
- food coloring (optional)

YOU DO:

1. Mix the flour and salt together in a bowl, using a spoon or your hands.

2. SLOWLY add the water, mixed with food coloring and oil (or detergent).

3 KNEAD the dough well and shape it into a ball. (For different colors, make several balls of plain dough and knead in the coloring.)

Put the remaining dough in a tightly closed container or plastic bag, and keep it in the refrigerator to be used again another day.

If it becomes too sticky, add more flour.

NOW YOU HAVE YOUR OWN PLAY DOUGH!

Enjoy rolling it, poking and pounding it, making it into people, animals, bowls, "cookies," "cakes," balls, holiday ornaments or other objects.

FOR ADDED FUN, use a rolling pin, a round block, a popsicle stick, cookie cutters, a plastic spoon or knife, bottle caps, a spool, etc. for rolling, cutting and decorating the dough.

MORE PLAY DOUGH

RUBBERY PLAYDOUGH
You Need:
• 2 cups baking soda
• 1½ cups water
• 1 cup cornstarch

You Do:
1. Mix with a fork until smooth.
2. Boil over moderate heat until thick (about a minute or so).
3. Spoon onto a plate or waxed paper.

NATURE'S PLAY DOUGH
You Need:
• 1 cup of flour
• ½ cup of salt
• 1 cup of water
• 2 tablespoons vegetable oil
• 2 tablespoons cream of tartar (optional)
• beet, spinach, and carrot juice

You Do:
1. Measure the flour, salt and oil and slowly add the water.
2. Cook over medium heat, stirring until the dough becomes stiff.
3. Turn out on waxed paper and let cool.
4. Knead the dough with your hands until it feels good.
5. Use as is, or divide into balls and add a few drops of the vegetable oil juices to make pink, green and orange.

BUMPY DOUGH
Add ¾ of a cup of flour to ¼ cup of salt; then mix with 2 or 3 teaspoons of water.

BREAD DOUGH
1. Cut the crusts off of slices of bread and mix with diluted white glue.
2. Form into shapes, animals, etc. When dry, paint and/or shellac.

PLAY CLAY

PLAY CLAY

Make up a large batch of play clay for hours of manipulative fun.

You Need:
- 6 cups of baking soda
- 3 cups of cornstarch
- 3½ cups of water
- ½ cup of salt

You Do:
1. Stir all of the ingredients together in a saucepan.
2. Cook on medium heat, stirring occasionally until the mixture bubbles and thickens.
3. Then spoon out onto a board, cover with a damp cloth and let cool.
4. Knead until smooth and divide into batches. Add food coloring, if you wish.
5. After using, store your clay in a tightly sealed plastic bag or a jar in the refrigerator. (Put a hole in small balls of clay and fill them with water before storing.)

Note: Play clay hardens slowly without baking and can be decorated with tempera or acrylic paint for a permanent finish.

COOKIE STAMPS

1. Roll small pieces of clay or fun dough into balls.
2. Pinch and pull out one end of the ball for a handle.
3. Flatten out the other end by tapping it down on the table.
4. Press in designs with a pencil, popsicle or orange stick. Make the imprints at least 1/8″ deep.
5. After the clay dries, bake it in a slow oven, or seal it with shellac or clear nail polish.

MORE PASTES

PAPIER – MÂCHÉ PASTE

You Need:
- ½ cup of non-rising wheat flour
- ¼ cup of powdered resin glue (available at hobby shops)
- ½ cup of warm water
- 1½ cups of hot water
- 4 drops of oil of wintergreen

You Do:
1. Mix the flour and resin glue in a saucepan.
2. Slowly pour in the warm water. Then add the hot water and stir vigorously.
3. Cook over low heat, stirring until the paste is smooth, thick and clear.

Note: This kind of paste should be used within 2 or 3 days. It will give a hard finish and works very well with large, permanent projects such as bowls, trays, candlesticks, large sculptures, etc.

PAPIER – MÂCHÉ PASTE #2

You Need:
- 1 cup of non-rising wheat flour
- ¼ cup of sugar
- 1 quart of warm water
- 1 quart of cold water
- ⅛ teaspoon of oil of wintergreen or oil of cinnamon

You Do
1. Mix together the flour and sugar in a saucepan.
2. Stir in a small amount of warm water.
3. Bring to a boil, stirring constantly and cook until thick and clear.
4. Add the oils, if not using immediately as a preservative.

Note: This is a good paste to use for strip mâché. It works best when still warm.

PAPERHANGER'S PASTE

You Need:
- 1 cup of non-rising wheat flour
- 1 tablespoon powdered alum
- 1 tablespoon powdered rosin
- 1½ cups of warm water
- 4½ cups of hot water
- 1½ cups of cold water
- 8 drops of oil of wintergreen, cloves or cinnamon

You Do:
1. Mix the flour, alum and rosin in a saucepan; then add the warm water, stirring until smooth.
2. Pour in the hot water and stir vigorously.
3. Place over low heat and boil until the paste becomes thick and clear.
4. Thin with the cold water.
5. Add the oil as a preservative, if not using immediately.

Note: This paste produces a hard finish and can be kept for several months. When using, reheat slightly. If too thick, thin with warm water. Excellent for making scrapbook covers, blocks from boxes, picture frames, etc.

"GUM" FOR STAMPS AND PAPER LABELS

You Need:
- 1 (¼ 3 ounce packet) of unflavored gelatin
- 1 tablespoon of cold water
- 3 tablespoons boiling water
- ½ teaspoon white peppermint extract
- 2 drops of boric acid solution

You Do:
1. Sprinkle the gelatin into the cold water to soften.
2. Pour into the boiling water, stirring until dissolved.
3. Add the remaining ingredients and mix well.

To use the glue, brush it thinly onto the back of a stamp or some paper and let dry. When applying to paper, just moisten it a bit. To keep, store the gel in a small jar or bottle with a lid. Warm in a pan to turn it into a liquid again!

PAINT, PAINT, PAINT

MAKE YOUR OWN PAINTS
You Need:
- ½ cup laundry starch
- ½ cup cold water
- 4 cups boiling water
- 1 tablespoon glycerin (drugstores carry this)
- powdered tempera paints

You Do:
1. Mix together the starch and water, and slowly pour in the boiling water, stirring with a long wooden spoon.
2. Add the glycerin and let cool.
3. Pour the paint mixture into small tin cans, baby food jars or a muffin tin and add a different color of tempera paint (food coloring also works) to each one. You could also pour thinned paint into squeeze bottles or into empty roll-on deodorant containers.
4. Store in the refrigerator, tightly covered, between painting sessions.

GOUACHE PAINT
(an opaque paint that dries quickly and can be painted on in layers).

You Need:
- 2 cups of dextrin (available at Hobby stores)
- 4 tablespoons distilled water
- ½ cup of honey
- 2 teaspoons glycerin
- ½ teaspoon boric acid solution
- powdered or poster paints

You Do:
1. Dissolve the dextrin in the water. (It will be slightly foamy.)
2. Then add the honey, glycerin and boric acid.
3. Stir well, or shake in a covered jar.
4. Mix this base with poster or powdered paint and store tightly covered.
5. Thin with water, if too thick.

TEMPERA EASEL PAINT

Add "Bentonite Extender" to powdered
tempera paint for an excellent
paint to use while working at an easel.

To make the extender:
You Need:
- 1 cup Bentonite (available in powder form
  at most art supply stores)
- ½ cup soap powder
- 2 quarts of water

You Do:
1. Mix well with an eggbeater or in a blender.
2. Let stand in a plastic or ceramic container
   for 2-3 days, stirring once each day.

To make the easel paint in large quantities
1. Mix together 6-8 tablespoons of the extender with a one pound
   container of powdered tempera, 3 cups of liquid starch, 2 tablespoons of soap flakes and a little water.
2. Beat until fluffy with an egg beater or blender. Add more water if
   too thick.
3. Store in a tightly covered container, pouring out what you need
   for each art session.

Quick paint ideas
Mix powdered tempera paint with:
1. Water and soap flakes to make it easier to wash out.
2. Detergent to prevent cracking.
3. Liquid starch to make it thicker.
4. Condensed milk for a glossy look.
5. Alum as a preservative.
6. Sawdust, salt, crushed eggshells, coffee grounds, crushed pasta
   bits, to give texture.

"OIL" PAINT PICTURES

1. Mix together powdered tempera paint and liquid detergent until it is thick and creamy.
2. Dip a knife or popsicle stick into the paint and spread it on paper in globs.

3. When the paint is dry, put on one or two more layers until your finished drawing looks just like a thick oil painting.

IMPASTO

1. Mix tempera paint with liquid starch until it is thick and fluffy.
2. Brush a thick layer of the paint over a piece of dark construction paper.
3. Using a plastic or cardboard fork, draw designs through the paint (you could also try other objects such as a paper clip, comb, wadded up newspaper, a popsicle stick, etc., to make textures).
4. If you want to do another design, just paint over the surface and begin again.

Variation: Using 3 colors of paint: red, yellow and blue, dip a cardboard comb in one of the paints and pull it across the paper to make straight, curvy, twisting, connected or disconnected lines. Keep doing this until your paper is filled with interesting, three—color designs.

FROSTY PICTURES

1. Whip up ⅔ cup of soapflakes and ⅓ cup of water and add a few drops of tempera paint or food coloring (or leave white for doing snow or cloud pictures).
2. To make a frosty picture, draw a winter scene on a piece of light blue or gray construction paper with your crayons. Press hard to get a waxy build up and leave a few places bare.
3. Dip a sponge into your fluffy paint and daub it on the picture to look like snow.

Another kind of a snow picture can be made by crayoning a picture on colored construction paper, then painting over it with a mixture of epsom salt and water (equal parts of each). As the water dries, watch the snowy crystals appear!

COLLAGE PAINTING

Mix rock salt, crushed egg shells and macaroni and other pasta with a powder paint and water and pour into a shaker. Cover a small area of your paper with some white glue thinned with water, then shake on the textured paint.

SPRINKLE A PAINTING

Sprinkle dry powdered paint and cornmeal over an area painted with thinned white glue. Shake off any excess paint.

SPACKLE ART

This is similar to plaster of Paris but is easier to use, as it dries much more slowly.

1. Mix spackling powder (found at hardware stores) with water until it is stiff like whipped cream - and not lumpy.
2. Then stir in your powdered paint.

Here are two ideas to do with Spackle Paint.

1. Pour several inches of the paint into a styrofoam food tray or a large plastic lid to make a hand or foot print or a plaque; then press in twigs, leaves, weeds, shells, crayon bits, to make a textured nature "picture."
2. Pour a glob of the spackle mixture onto wax paper and press in a variety of collage materials. Wait for about an hour for the spackle to dry, then lift off the wax paper.

MORE PAINT IDEAS

1. Mix together salt and powdered tempera and pour into a shaker or muffin tin. To "paint" a picture, just sprinkle or shake over **wet** paper.
2. Pour thin tempera paint into a clothes sprinkle-bottle or shaker and gently shake it over a piece of **dry** paper.
3. Make a **"spatter painting"** by using an old toothbrush to spray the paint through a piece of screening onto paper. This is particularly effective with leaves, weeds, flowers or cut out stencils.
4. For a 3-D look, mix 1 cup of powdered detergent and ½ cup of liquid starch. Whip with an egg beater and divide into batches. Then stir in some powdered tempera paint. Use this mixture to make 3-D maps and pictures, just like you would salt and flour.

PAINTING POINTERS

1. Spread out an old vinyl tablecloth on the floor and you'll have a **special** place for drawing and painting. Your "magic carpet" will be perfect for doing anything messy like fun dough and finger painting, since any spills can easily be washed up with a sponge and some water.

2. A **plastic smock** or an **old shirt** of Dad's (or Mom's) will protect your clothes from spills.

3. Use a store-bought **easel,** or make your own from cardboard or masonite; or spread an old **vinyl tablecloth** on the floor.

4. Paint on **large sheets** of newsprint, manila or grey bogus paper, cut-up grocery bags, newspapers, or pages from sample wall paper books. Paintings done on pieces of **corrugated** cardboard are really fun. Apply the paint, then watch the different colors "mix together" in the grooves!

5. **Brushes** with long handles and wide, stiff bristles are best for young artists. Brush across the paper in long strokes; splatter the paint by tapping the handle; twist, press, and roll the bristles. If you stick a small wad of foil or a cut-off plastic drinking straw through the middles of the brush, the bristle will split into two parts and your paint will make **double** lines on the paper. When you are finished painting, clean your brushes with **soap** and **cold water.** Store, bristles up, in a coffee can - or wrap in newspaper. Sponges, feathers, an old comb, cardboard strips with "teeth" cut into one edge also are fun for experimenting.

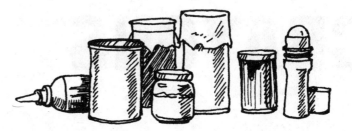

6. Cans, jars, milk cartons, a plastic egg carton or a muffin tin make **handy containers** for your paint.
7. Plastic **squeeze bottles** (from mustard, liquid soap, etc.) or roll-top plastic deodorant bottles make nifty storage containers, and you'll enjoy squeezing out or rolling on the paint.

8. To make tempera paint into a **thin wash,** use three parts water to one part paint.
9. For a **thick, foamy paint** that will cover plastic milk and egg cartons and other slick surfaces, mix tempera paint with soapflakes or liquid detergent and beat with an egg beater until fluffy.

10. A few drops of **oil of wintergreen** or **cinnamon** will give your paint a pleasant smell.
11. For a **"throw-away" palette** for thick tempera paint or acrylics, attach several sheets of waxed paper to a piece of heavy cardboard. Then **peel off** the top layer when you are ready to clean up.

12. To keep the **lids** of storage jars from **sticking,** grease them with cold cream or vaseline.

13. Brush or spray on lacquer, clear plastic or varnish to keep your finished chalked or painted pictures bright. Hang wet paintings over a wire or clothesline, or on a drying rack. Those with heavy paint should be dried **flat** on newspapers on a table or the floor. You can press out any wrinkles with a warm iron. (Place the painting between two sheets of thick paper or newspaper.)

14. An empty **six-pack carton** from cold drinks or a plastic fishing-tackle box, make a handy **carry-all** for your supplies.

CRAYONS

CRAYON FUN

To make your own crayons:

1. Put pieces of old crayons of the same and similar colors in a coffee can and set it in a pan of water on the stove. Cook until the crayons melt.
2. Pour the wax into a mold (a cardboard tube or something smaller) and let harden.

SHAVED CRAYON PICTURES

1. Sprinkle crayon shavings on a piece of waxed paper.
2. Cover with another piece, put between layers of newspaper and press with a warm iron.
3. Frame with construction paper and hang up in a window.

Note: Be sure a grown-up helps with these projects.

CHALK

MAKE YOUR OWN CHALK

1. Mix together 2 tablespoons of powdered tempera paint, ½ cup of water and 3 tablespoons of plaster of Paris.
2. Pour the mixture into a small paper cup and let harden.
3. After an hour or so, peel off the cup.

For a home-made **chalk-board**, spray several coats of special chalk board paint (sold at hobby or paint stores) on a piece of cardboard. When dry, border the edges with colorful cloth tape.

CHALK IDEAS

1. Wet your paper and let the chalk stick **glide** over it; or dip the chalk into water and draw on dry paper. Soak the paper under the faucet or with a sponge – smooth it out on a table or the floor. You can also soak your chalk sticks in a glass of water and rub them on the paper. Blur the colors together with your fingers. Your chalked picture will look just like paint.

2. Paint over the paper with **liquid starch.** Then make designs on the wet paper with your colored chalks. When your picture dries, the chalk won't rub off.

3. Place a spoonful of **buttermilk** in the center of fingerpaint paper or a damp paper towel; then fold the paper in half, pressing all over it with your hands. Now chalk a picture, and your chalk stick will slip and slide over the surface.

4. To make **colorful chalk cut-outs** of shapes, flowers, easter eggs, etc., wet a piece of paper and color all over it with your chalk, using one or more colors. After the paper dries, draw and cut out **shapes** and glue them onto a piece of colored construction paper.

5. Make chalk **rubbings** by placing your paper over bumpy surfaces like sandpaper, corrugated cardboard, hard plastic meat trays, paper clips, a doilie, and so forth.

6. Pour **sawdust** or sand, chalk **shavings,** and tempera paint into a bowl. Cover with water and let stand for 6 to 8 hours. Then sprinkle the mixture on **glued areas** of paper or cardboard like a **sandpainting.**

7. Ask permission to use wet chalk outdoors on a **window.** Draw a picture, using several colors, or chalk over the entire pane and do a fingerpainting. When you're finished, just wipe off the chalk with a damp cloth or a paper towel. Go over it again with a crumpled newspaper, and the window will be **sparkly clean!**

PICTURE COLLAGES

YOU NEED:
- Paper, cardboard or a food tray
- Yarn or string
- Macaroni, beans, • Scissors
  rice or cereal • Crayons
- Popsicle sticks • Paste/glue
- Cloth and paper scraps
- Newspapers and magazines

YOU DO:

1. Tear paper into SMALL pieces and paste them down on cardboard, construction paper or a food tray.

2. Next, tear and paste down LARGER SHAPES to look like people, animals or objects. Can you make a BUNNY with long, pointed ears? How about a jack-o-lantern, or a house with smoke coming out of the chimney?

3. Torn pieces from newspaper comics and magazine pages make COLORFUL collages. For a black, gray and white effect, tear shapes from the NEWS or the CLASSIFIED ADS. Collages of WORDS are fun to make.

4. Or··· CUT construction paper shapes and paste them onto a sheet of paper; try cloth shapes, too.

5. Add ODDS 'N ENDS from the pantry, along with straws, popsicle sticks, and yarn, to make a picture. Use your crayons for outlines or to fill in open spaces.

6. For a FRAME, fold a piece of paper in half; then tear or cut out the middle.

22 If you used a food tray, your picture is all ready to hang!

EGG CARTON SORTERS

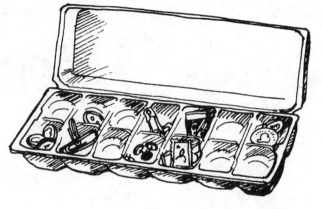

1. Turn an egg carton upside down, punch holes in the "bumps", and you'll have a handy place to store scissors, crayons, markers, etc.

2. Turn a carton right side up to keep all of your ODDS 'N ENDS for craft projects: cloth and paper scraps, beads, shells ···

3. Wrap and store handmade Easter eggs or Christmas tree ornaments, each in its own compartment.

4. Keep your SEWING supplies organized and handy: needles, spools of thread, buttons, snaps, hooks, safety pins ···

5. Use the inside sections to hold various sized nails, screws and bolts for your carpentry projects, or to serve as a SORTING BOX for stamps, coins, paper clips, brads and so forth.

6. A decorated jewelry box would make a thoughtful gift. Cover with bright paper and glue on pictures, shells, buttons, macaroni, etc.

Egg cartons also make handy THROW-AWAY CONTAINERS for glue or paint!

ZOO SKETCHING

...can be fun and educational too, if you sketch what you see.

YOU NEED:
- Crayons, chalk or pencils
- Cardboard for a drawing board
- Paper

YOU DO:

1. Tour the zoo, CAREFULLY OBSERVING all of the animals and birds.

2. Then go back and DRAW your favorite one. What shape is its head and body? Does it have any special features, such as horns, antlers, pouches?

3. What color is it? One or several? Is the hair on its body curly or straight? Or none at all? Any feathers or spots?

4. You may want to FRAME each animal picture with construction paper... or put several birds or animals into a large MURAL.

5. Add zoo "scenery" to your mural: benches, trees cages, signs, food stands... or even a children's train.

BOXY SCULPTURES

YOU NEED:

- Boxes and containers of all shapes and sizes
- Cardboard tubes
- Egg cartons
- Wood scraps
- Paint
- Scissors
- Construction paper
- Crayons
- Glue or tape
- Cloth scraps, buttons, yarn, etc.

YOU DO:

1. You can create animals, people or free-form constructions by gluing or taping together all kinds of boxes, cartons and tubes.

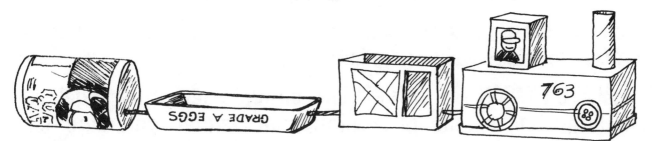

2. Decorate your sculpture with paint, crayons or construction paper. Add buttons, beans, beads, shells, cloth scraps and other odds and ends.

3. You can make fascinating junk sculptures out of all the scrap materials you've been collecting. For added fun, make it a group project!

TIN CAN CREATURES

YOU NEED:

- Several tin cans in graduated sizes
- String or elastic thread
- Paint or markers
- Spools, lids
- Buttons, beads
- Glue • Yarn
- Hammer • Nail

YOU DO:

1. Be sure the cans are shiny clean!

2. Punch holes (using a nail and hammer) and STRING the cans together to make various animal shapes.

3. To make a DRAGON or CATERPILLAR, string a few cans together from largest to smallest. Fashion pipe cleaner antennae for the caterpillar. Glue on paper "stripes" or "spots," and make hair and tails of yarn or fringed paper.

4. Fill some of the cans with rice, beans, bottlecaps or bells, and tape them shut for SOUND EFFECTS.

5. Use spools, spray can lids, or even milk carton sections, along with the cans. You could make a jointed puppet — or anything you can dream up!

26

EGG CARTON TOTEM POLES

Egg cartons can be used for almost any kind of creative craft project — from flowers and bells to creepy caterpillars or alligator puppets to learning games or a totem pole.

TOTEM POLE

1. Take your egg carton and carefully cut down the middle so you have two long pieces.

2. Wind several rubber bands around the top, middle and bottom.

3. Decorate it all the way around; and insert wings, cut from the carton lid, between the sections.

4. For a stand, use 4 egg cups, a small box or a styrofoam block.

YOUNGER CHILDREN can just decorate the "bumps" on the bottom of the carton, then tape on wings cut from the carton lid.

FUN WITH SCISSORS

1. Cut some paper – any way you wish – making straight or curvy shapes of all sizes.

2. Fringe the edges of a paper placemat....

3. Draw wavy lines on a piece of paper. Practice cutting SHAPES by holding the scissors STILL and moving the paper you are cutting to follow an outline. Maybe you can cut a curlique or a "thing-a-ma-jig."

4. Cut out strips of colored paper. Paste them onto paper of a contrasting color — then paste on stars in a "helter-skelter" pattern.

5. Cut the corners off of square pieces of colored paper to make CIRCLES. Then fringe the edges and paste them onto a large piece of paper in a design. Maybe a Spring "shower" will emerge — or "flowers," if you add on stems and leaves.

6. Cut thin strips of crepe paper. Roll each strip into a small ball and paste onto a sheet of cardboard in a pattern to form a MOSAIC.

What else can you cut, fringe, fold, crumple, paste and design?

28

CUT-OUT DESIGNS

YOU NEED:

- One 9"x 12" piece of construction paper
- One 6"x 9" piece of another color
- Scissors
- Paste or glue

YOU DO:

1. Fold a 6"x 9" piece of colored construction paper in half, lengthwise.

2. Hold the open edges, and cut various shapes out of the folded edge.

3. Open the paper and paste it onto one half of the large piece of paper.

4. On the other side paste on the cut-out shapes, in the same order. (See illustration.)

5. You'll have a picture with two panels; one positive and one negative. Add to the design if you wish.

Adapted from <u>Arts & Crafts Discovery Units</u> by Jenean Romberg. Used with permission.

PAPER ANIMALS

YOU NEED:
- Construction paper
- Scissors
- Glue or tape
- Round objects
- Crayons or markers

YOU DO:
1. Make all kinds of animals by cutting, rolling and taping together paper shapes. Roll large and small RECTANGLES into cylinders or TUBES. Then, glue or tape them together.

2. Draw and cut out CIRCLES by tracing around a jar lid, cup or glass. Make a slit to the center and overlap the ends to form a CONE. Glue or tape together.

3. Cut out TRIANGLES and fold them down the middle for ears and beaks.

4. Use long, thin STRIPS of paper to make curls by rolling them around a pencil. Or, cut slits in the end of a wider strip for FRINGE.

5. Now take ALL of your PAPER SHAPES and glue or tape them together into all kinds of funny animals. Use the large tubes for the bodies, the smaller ones for legs and arms. Then add a head, ears, tail, mane and so forth.

6. Use your crayons or markers to make eyes, spots, stripes, zigzags and other features and decorations.

PAPER PUPPETS

YOU NEED:
- Construction paper or cardboard tubes
- Scissors
- Crayons or markers
- Paste or glue
- Popsicle sticks or cardboard tubes from wire hangers

YOU DO:
1. Cut out people or animals from construction paper (or draw directly on the tube).

2. Draw or paste on eyes, ears, teeth, hair, clothes, etc.

3. Attach a popsicle stick or long tube to the back of each puppet for a handle.

BEEHIVE HAT

YOU NEED:

- Corrugated paper
- Tape measure
- Scissors
- Tape
- Paint, crayons or markers

YOU DO:

1. Cut the corrugated paper into strips about 1½" wide.

2. Tape the strips together to form one long piece. (You will need about **6** feet all together.) Roll the strip into a circle and tape down the end.

3. Measure AROUND the outside of the circle to be sure it will fit your head. If not, add on more strips.

4. Gently pull up the center of the roll until you have a CONE shape. Push the strips in and out to form the **SHAPE** you want.

5. Turn the hat over and reinforce the "inside" of it with long pieces of tape, so the strips will stay in place.

6. Paint your hat, if you wish. Or add a feather or flower, or even some tiny bees.

SPRINGY CREATURES

YOU NEED:
- Paper
- Scissors
- Paste
- Crayons

YOU DO:

1. Cut out circles and ovals for the head, body, hands and feet. Add features and clothes, if you wish.

2. Make as many "springs"✳ as you need for arms, legs, tails, etc.

3. Assemble your "creature" by pasting the ends of the springs onto the body parts.

Suggestions: a springly cat for Halloween, a bouncy Santa, a leggy leprechaun, a jack-in-the-box..

Paste here

✳ HOW TO MAKE "SPRINGS"

1. Paste together, at right angles, two strips of paper of the same length.

2. Fold UP strip A; fold strip B to the LEFT. Then fold DOWN strip A and fold to the RIGHT strip B. Keep folding until you come to the end of the strips.

33

GADGET PRINTING

YOU NEED:

- Gadgets to print with : sticks, corks, spools, hair rollers, egg carton cups, bits of sponge, an eraser, a dried corncob, etc.

- Vegetables, like a potato, carrot or turnip; orange or grapefruit half, scooped-out

- Jar lids, pans or a muffin tin

- Tempera paint
- All kinds of paper

- Newspaper, paper towels

Potato Print

carrot print

YOU DO:

1. Spread newspapers over your work area.

2. Cut a design into a potato, carrot, eraser, etc. (Have an adult help with this.)

3. Pour a SMALL amount of paint into a jar lid or muffin tin.

4. Dip your vegetable, or one of the other objects, into the paint (you may need to BLOT it first on a paper towel or newspaper); then PRESS it down on your paper.

5. Print a PATTERN by repeating the design over and over. You can make wrapping paper, notepaper, greeting cards, or a picture.

STYROFOAM PRINTS

YOU NEED:

- Styrofoam grocery trays
- Pencil or ball point pen
- Tempera paint • Paper
- Paint brush or roller
- Scissors • Glue

YOU DO:

1. Cut off the edges of a styrofoam tray.

2. Draw a **DESIGN OR PICTURE** on the **SMOOTH** side of the tray, pressing down hard with a pencil or ball point pen. (Remember: letters and words must be written **BACKWARDS**, from right to left.)

3. Next, cover your picture with paint.

4. Then, carefully lay a piece of paper **OVER** the painted surface. Smooth over it several times with your hand.

5. Now, **PULL OFF** the paper and you will see your picture in print! (The indented lines will resist the paint and remain the color of the paper.) This is a good way to make holiday cards for family and friends.

6. **VARIATIONS:**

   - Experiment by using several colors. When the "printing plate" is dry, apply more paint to make more prints.

   - Crayon printing — Place a sheet of lightweight paper over the "plate" and rub with the side of a crayon. Repeat a small design by moving your paper several times (to make a pattern).

MAKE A COLOR WHEEL

YOU NEED:

- 1 small plain paper plate
  1 large plain paper plate
  (or cardboard circles)
- Crayons
- Felt tip markers
- Brad fastener
- Ruler   • Pencil

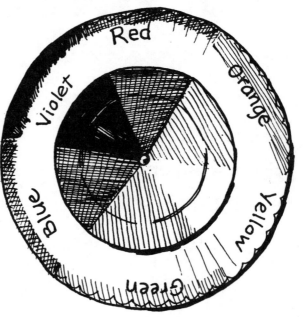

YOU DO:

1. Divide the SMALL paper plate or cardboard circle into SIX EQUAL sections. Make the sections the following colors IN ORDER: red, orange, yellow, green, blue and violet.

2. Then divide a LARGE paper plate into six equal sections. Write the NAME of the color at the top of each section and color the outside edge to match — follow the same order as the small plate.

3. Fasten the small plate to the large one with a brad in the center. Spin to match the colors on the plates.

The PRIMARY colors are red, yellow and blue.

The SECONDARY colors are orange, green and violet.

The colors next to each other are ANALOGOUS (or "friends"). Can you name each color and its "friends"?

The colors across from each other are COMPLEMENTARY: red—green, yellow—violet, and blue—orange.

RAINBOW RHYMES

THE RAINBOW

The rainbow arches in the sky,
But in the earth it ends;
And if you ask the reason why,
They'll tell you "That depends."

It never comes without the rain,
Nor goes without the sun;
And tho you try with might and main,
You'll never catch me one.

by David McCord

YELLOW

Green is go,
and red is stop,
and yellow is peaches
with cream on top.

Earth is brown,
and blue is sky;
yellow looks well
on a butterfly.

Clouds are white,
black, pink, or mocha;
yellow's a dish of
tapioca.

by David McCord
Reprinted with permission

RAINBOW RHYMES

Rainbows upside-down;
  are like
    smiles
      rightside-up.

Red and orange,
  green and blue,
    shiny yellow,
  purple, too.
All the colors
  that you know
    up in
  the rainbow.

Friends are like rainbows.
They bring laughter to
your eyes.

Tom Klika
Rainbows St. Martin's Press, 1979.
Reprinted with permission

CRAYON EXPERIMENTS

RAINBOWS – Hold 2 or 3 crayons together in your hand. Press them down on your paper and make straight, curved and squiggly lines.

EXPERIMENTS – Peel the paper wrappers off and use the side of the crayon to color in large areas. Experiment with SHORT and LONG strokes; make LIGHT and HEAVY ones, too.
Go over some parts again, pressing hard to make the color darker. Try coloring over a light color like yellow with a blue or green crayon.

SGRAFFITO (etching) – Begin by COVERING a small piece of paper completely with several colors of crayon (press down hard). Then color over the entire surface with a BLACK CRAYON.
Now, scratch through the black layer with a pointed object (toothpick, hairpin, nail, etc.), exposing the bright colors underneath.

MAGIC PICTURES – First, DRAW a picture or design, pressing firmly with your crayons. Then, PAINT over the area and see what happens. (The crayon areas will RESIST the paint.)

MORE MAGIC – Experiment by drawing with a BLACK crayon on black paper; then cover the surface with thin white paint. (Try white on white with dark paint.) Watch the MAGIC PICTURE appear!

KID'S CLEAN-UP

It's a breeze to clean up
   any mess you might make,
When working with paint,
   paste or clay.

Newpapers spread out
   beneath where you work,
Can be crumpled and
   thrown right away.

A sponge and a rag and some water —
   in a pail or a nearby sink,
Will make your clean-up really a breeze,
   and quicker than you might think.

But working outdoors
   is the best place of all,
You can just use the hose—
   or the next big rainfall!

                                    cbh

JUNK

Junk, junk, beautiful junk
   will provide hours of creative play.
Tubes and boxes, cardboard and paper,
   to keep you happy and busy each day.

Spools and buttons, yarn and ribbon,
   popsicle sticks and clay,
Save them **all** in a large carton or bag—
   don't ever throw them away!

                                    cbh

LEARNING WITH BOXES

This direction game will help you understand POSITION WORDS: on, into, over, around, under

YOU NEED:

2 large boxes
(1 of them open at both ends, and 1 with just the top open)

YOU DO:

1. Play the game by following directions, such as: climb INTO the box; peek AROUND the box; crawl THROUGH the box; stand BETWEEN the two boxes; put a toy ON TOP OF the box; put a toy IN the box; look for a surprise UNDER the box.

2. Now open one of the boxes completely and make it into a long RAMP. Place the ramp over some pillows to make a bridge, or spread it out on the floor to use as a sidewalk. Now walk along the sidewalk. Walk back and forth several times, then try hopping, jumping, putting one foot in front of the other, and so forth. Jump OVER the sidewalk. Roll a ball or small toy truck or car ALONG the sidewalk.

FUN WITH BLOCKS

YOU DO:

1. Make your own blocks by stuffing large GROCERY BAGS with crumpled up pieces of newspaper. Tape the tops securely.

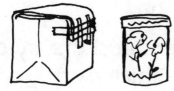

2. Stuff boxes, of different sizes and shapes, with crumpled newspaper. Tape down the top and edges, and cover with contact paper or brightly colored magazine pictures. Protect with clear contact paper or spray with shellac. Include some round boxes and some milk cartons.

3. Find large pieces of wood at the lumberyard (most have a scrap pile); or saw 2×4's and dowels of various sizes. Sand well and varnish for a smooth, lasting finish.

HAVE FUN building: houses, apartment buildings, garages, towers, walls, roads, villages and anything else you can think up!

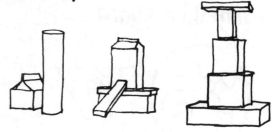

SHAPES & COLORS

YOU NEED:

- Poster board in four different colors
- Scissors
- A stapler

PUZZLES

1. Cut out the four basic shapes (a circle, square, triangle and rectangle) from 4 different colors of poster board.

2. Cut each shape up into five or six pieces (like a puzzle)

3. Mix up all the pieces, then put each color together again.

POCKETS

1. Cut out 5 shapes from the poster board; a circle, square, triangle, rectangle and octagon.

2. Make pockets by cutting out and stapling on ½ of each shape, as shown in the picture.

3. Put different objects into each pocket, like crayons, a ruler, a stick puppet, a cookie...

4. Then give DIRECTIONS: "pull out the ruler from the triangle", "count the crayons in the circle", "add another puppet to the octagon", "eat the cookie..."

SHAPE LOTTO

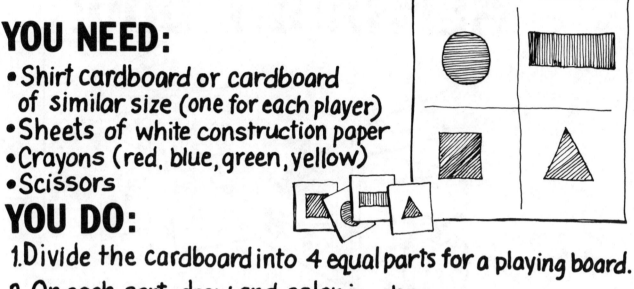

YOU NEED:
- Shirt cardboard or cardboard of similar size (one for each player)
- Sheets of white construction paper
- Crayons (red, blue, green, yellow)
- Scissors

YOU DO:

1. Divide the cardboard into 4 equal parts for a playing board.

2. On each part, draw and color in shapes:
   - ○ a red circle
   - △ a blue triangle
   - ▨ a green square
   - ▭ a yellow rectangle

3. Make 16 "PLAYING CARDS" by cutting construction paper into small squares and drawing one of the above shapes on each... in corresponding colors. (Make 4 cards with red circles, 4 with blue triangles, etc.)

4. Shuffle cards and lay them face down. As each player draws one in turn, he matches the shape on the card to the one on the board and covers it. If the shape is already covered, he turns the card face down on the bottom of the pile.

5. The first child to cover all 4 shapes on his card is THE WINNER!

★ FOR VARIATION: Draw 4 OBJECTS on the cardboard and put RELATED OBJECTS on the cards — comb and brush, pen and pencil, gas pump and car, etc.

FOLD-OUT
ALPHABET BOOK

1. To make the book, TAPE the pieces of cardboard together, leaving a little SPACE between the edges.

2. Bend the pages back and forth like an accordion.

3. On each page, put a large ALPHABET LETTER...in sequence.

4. Find and cut out PICTURES to go with each letter (or draw them). For example: A - artichoke or apple
   B - bird or bear
   C - cucumber or cake
   D - doll or dog

5. Talk about each picture. Say the letter and then the name.

6. Go from the beginning to the end of the book, reciting each letter of the alphabet.
   "... Now I know my A B C's
   Oh, how happy I will be!"

BUTTON-ON BOOK

YOU NEED:
- Cardboard or styrofoam from food trays
- Stiff cloth (for the pages of your book)
- Felt scraps
- Buttons of different sizes
- Scissors
- Crayons

YOU DO:

1. Make GIANT "paper dolls" out of styrofoam trays or cardboard. Color the hair and draw in the face.

2. Sew buttons on the dolls in appropriate places as shown in the illustration. Then glue the dolls onto cloth pages.

3. Cut out articles of clothing for the dolls from felt: a dress, jeans, a vest, a blouse or shirt, a hat.

4. Everywhere there is a button on the doll, cut a slit in the felt a little larger than the button.

5. Now dress the dolls by buttoning on each article of clothing where it belongs.

45

SHOEBOX NUMBER GAMES

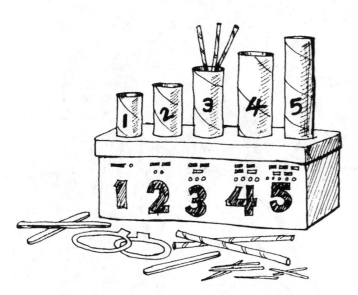

YOU NEED:
- A shoe box, with a lid
- Cardboard tubes
- Construction or contact paper (optional)
- Scissors • Glue • Markers
- Six-pak rings • Popsicle sticks
- Plastic straws
- Felt or sandpaper

YOU DO:

1. Cut the tubes into 4 or 5 different lengths. Number them from 1 to 5, beginning with the shortest.

2. Glue each tube onto the box lid, according to **size**.

3. Cover the box with construction or contact paper, if you wish; then put on the lid.

4. Poke holes and/or slits in the side of the box to correspond with the **numbers** on the tubes. (You'll need help with this.)

5. Paste on sandpaper or felt numbers under the holes and slits. Now you are ready for some number games •••

RING TOSS - Cut apart the six-pak rings. Then play a ring toss game, seeing how **high** your score will be.

COUNT-UPS - Push toothpicks into the holes and popsicle sticks through the slits, **counting** as you go. Place the correct number of straws into each tube.

FEELIES - Run your fingers over the felt or sandpaper numbers and **FEEL** the shape. **SAY** the number, too.

KITCHEN COUNTERS

YOU NEED:

- Shirt cardboard or construction paper
- Scissors
- Glue
- Crayons
- Pantry odds and ends... dried cereal, beans, macaroni, toothpicks, bottle caps, cut-up straws, etc.

YOU DO:

1. Cut cardboard or paper into large squares to make your "COUNTING CARDS."

2. Glue ONE ITEM (i.e. a jar lid) on the first card and write the number 1 on the back of the card.

3. Glue TWO ITEMS (i.e. 2 pieces of macaroni) on the second card and write the number 2 on the back.

4. Make as many cards as you wish with the appropriate number of items on each.

A GAME FOR 2 OR MORE CHILDREN
Using your own set of cards, take turns matching, counting or guessing the correct numbers. 47

EGG CARTON

LEARNING BOX

YOU NEED:

- egg carton
- scissors
- glue
- large beans
- cardboard or construction paper
- bottle caps or buttons
- magazine or newspaper pictures

YOU DO:

1. Make matching sets of any or all of the following:

1 2 3 4 5 6 7 8 9 10 11 12 numbers

A B C D E F G H I J K L M N O P Q R S T U V W X Y Z alphabet

▲ ● ◻ ▦ ◖ ◣ ◆ ☾ colored shapes

🐰 ★ 🌳 🌙 👢 🔑 🖼 📺 😊 🍀 🚗 🦋 pictures of everyday objects

2. Glue ONE SET of items onto various parts of the egg carton.. all sections are usable, inside and out. Put the numbers inside the egg cups for counting.

3. Now match the OTHER SET of letters, shapes, numbers, etc. to those attached to your box. (The letters and numbers can be glued to buttons or bottle caps for STURDIER markers.)

4. Use the beans to PRACTICE COUNTING: place one in cup #1, two in cup #2, etc.

CAN YOU THINK OF OTHER WAYS TO USE YOUR LEARNING BOX?

PLAY AND LEARN
SALT BOX

YOU NEED:

- A baking pan, old dishpan or a large shallow box
- Salt, cornmeal or sand (Kosher salt is best.)
- Unbreakable kitchen items: bowl, funnel, measuring cups, spoons . . .
- Popsicle sticks, straws and toothpicks
- Rubber bands, curtain rings, cardboard or plastic circles
- Newspapers or plastic cloth

YOU DO:

1. Fill the container about 3/4 full of sand or salt. Then enjoy trying some of the following activities:
   - Practice writing NUMBERS and ALPHABET LETTERS with your fingers or a stick.
   - Can you spell out your name? your friend's? your cat's or dog's? Do a few easy addition and subtraction problems. Play tic-tac-toe with a friend...
   - Draw PICTURES — to "erase", gently shake the box; then start all over again!
   - Make CONSTRUCTIONS by stacking up and crisscrossing toothpicks, straws or popsicle sticks.
   - Play a RINGTOSS game by tossing cardboard or plastic circles over the toothpicks and straws.

2. Use your box for all kinds of CREATIVE PLAY — make 3-D villages, adding tiny cars, animals and people to go along your roads and walkways.

LET'S GO FISHING

YOU NEED:
- A stick, ruler or cardboard tube from a hanger
- Construction paper
- String
- Magnet
- Scissors
- Box
- Crayons
- Paper clips

YOU DO:

1. For a fishing pole, tie one end of a long string to a stick or tube. Attach a magnet to the other end.

2. Cut out several FISH from construction paper. Color them and write a letter or number on each.

3. Next fasten a PAPER CLIP at the mouth of each fish.

4. Make a FISH POND from a box and place all your fish inside.

5. Now with your pole TRY TO CATCH A FISH! (The magnet will attract the paper clip.) What number or letter did you catch? What color is it?

VARIATIONS

Make up games for 2 or more children.

See who can catch the fish with the highest number or the one with the blue dot, etc.

Look in a book and find different kinds of fish and try to draw them. See who can guess their names.

Write a poem or limerick on each fish. Older children can read them to each other.

Make a FOLD-OUT fish with a math problem, a riddle, or any QUESTION on the outside... and the ANSWER on the inside.

LEARNING TREE

YOU NEED:

- A large piece of cardboard or paper
- Crayons • Scissors
- Tape • Glue
- PICTURES from magazines and OBJECTS such as buttons, ribbons, sticks, etc

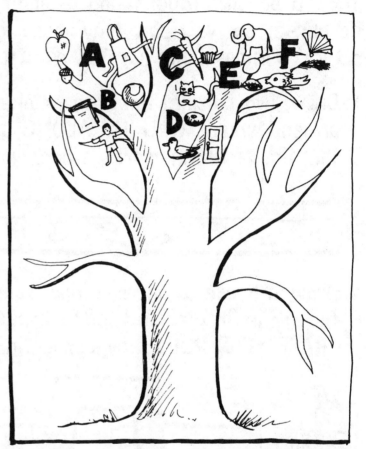

YOU DO:

1. Draw or paste a LARGE TREE on the cardboard. Color if you wish.

2. Each day choose a different letter of the ALPHABET, beginning with A. Find pictures or objects that start with that letter: A - apple, auto, apron; B - button, book, beans, bottlecap, etc.

3. Glue the LETTER FOR THE DAY on the tree and tape the objects or pictures around it. Start in the upper left hand corner and go across the branches.

4. Several times during the day, say the letter and name the object.

5. After 26 days your tree will be filled with the **WHOLE** alphabet.

6. Recite the alphabet··· Can you make up a story using all of the words on your tree?

PENCIL & PAPER GAMES

Tuck a pencil, crayons and a small pad of paper in your pocket or purse, so you can play these games while waiting for the doctor, riding in the car or on a bus.

1. Draw two parallel lines, then take your crayon or pencil and pretend you're WALKING ALONG a balance board. Do it again, this time making marks where your feet would go.

2. Draw a house at one end and your school at the other (or a store, the movie theatre, a friend's house, the playground, etc.). Then TRACE YOUR ROUTE by connecting the two places.

3. Draw two WAVY lines and sail your boat along the ocean.

4. Can you guide your pencil along a ZIG-ZAGGY sidewalk? or up and down some tall mountains?

MORE PENCIL GAMES

5. SCATTER some dots on the paper and connect them. Do you see a design or picture?

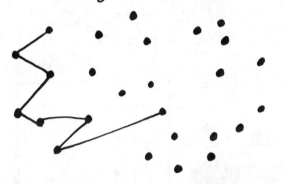

Put the dots into STRAIGHT ROWS and make boxes. Play the "box game" with a friend ⋯ take turns drawing ONE line and try to finish up a box. When you do, put your initial inside and take another turn. Who will have the most boxes?

6. Make a page of STRAIGHT lines; then think of groups of things like: sports, food, toys, animals and so forth. Draw pictures of them between 2 lines, being sure each one sits on the bottom line and touches the top line. Try letters, numbers and shapes, too.

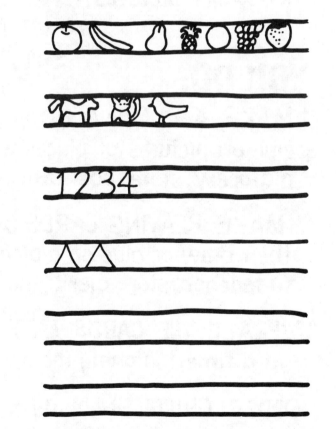

These games are also fun to play on a blackboard or sidewalk.

PEOPLE AT WORK

YOU NEED:

- Cardboard
- Crayons or pencil
- Glue • Scissors
- Construction paper
- Magazine and newspaper pictures

YOU DO:

1. MAKE A PLAYING BOARD out of cardboard. Draw or glue on pictures of places where people work (a school, a grocery store, post office, fire station, etc.).

2. MAKE PLAYING CARDS by cutting up paper or cardboard; then draw or glue on a picture of PEOPLE AT WORK (a teacher, store clerk, mailman, fireman, etc.).

3. PLACE THE CARDS FACE DOWN in a pile. Pick one at a time, matching the person to his place of work.

OLDER CHILDREN could make a larger playing board with more occupations: bakery...baker; police station... policeman or woman; bank...teller; department store... salesperson; hospital...doctor or nurse.

TREASURE HUNT

YOU NEED:

- Magazine or newspaper pictures
- Scissors
- Glue

YOU DO:

1. Plan an indoor TREASURE HUNT, using pictures of familiar HOUSEHOLD ITEMS (radio, lamp, refrigerator, chair, pillow, etc.) as clues.
2. Write out a list and hide 4-6 PICTURE CLUES around the house for the children to find.
3. Give the players PICTURE CLUE #1 (for example, a picture of a radio) and tell them to hunt for the item in the picture. On or under the radio they will find PICTURE CLUE #2 (perhaps a telephone) which will lead them to a 3rd clue ··· and so on.
4. The "hunters" MOVE IN ORDER, from clue to clue, until they have found the HIDDEN TREASURE! (A paperback book, cookies, a new ball, etc.)

FOR CHILDREN AGES 6-10: Use more clues or ones of RELATED rather than identical objects. Example: comb ··· brush, stamp ··· envelope Or make up a rhyme – "Look carefully everywhere, next to a lamp or under a chair."

On a nice day, try the treasure hunt OUTDOORS!

CROSSING STREETS

Stop on the corner
Watch for the light.
Look to the left,
Look to the right.

If nothing is coming,
Then start and don't talk.
Go straight across,
Be careful and walk.

When I walk home from school today
I'll walk the safe and careful way.
I'll look to the left—I'll look to the right.
Then cross the street when no car is in sight.

MY HOME IN THE SKY

My home in the sky is twelve stories high,
When I look out the window I can see
The tops of low buildings, cars, trees and tiny people
Hurrying by on the streets below.

STOP AND GO
A SAFETY GAME

YOU NEED:

- A large piece of cardboard and several smaller pieces
- Crayons or felt tipped pens
- Ruler • Scissors
- Buttons, bottle caps, stones, for markers, one for each player

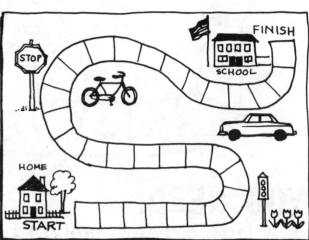

YOU DO:

1. DRAW A SIDEWALK of about 20 squares on the cardboard.

2. Draw (or glue on) a HOUSE for the "START" and a SCHOOL for the "FINISH". Add trees, cars, etc.

3. Make a set of GAME CARDS from small squares of cardboard or paper. Write a BASIC SAFETY RULE on each card (See samples below.) **or** paste on a picture.

4. Shuffle the cards and put them in a pile face down for each player TO DRAW IN TURN.

5. The first player to get to "SCHOOL" is the winner.

GO CARDS Make **4** of each	**WAIT CARDS** Make **2** of each	**STOP CARDS** Make **1** of each
1. You waited for a green light before crossing the street. Go ahead 2 spaces. 2. You looked both ways before crossing. Go ahead 3 spaces. 3. You held a small child's hand to help her across the street. Go ahead 2 spaces.	1. The light is yellow. **Wait** where you are. 2. Your bike has a flat tire. **Stay put.** 3. You cut through a neighbor's yard. **Wait** out your turn. 4. You forgot your lunch. **Go back home!**	1. The light is red! **Stop** and stay where you are. 2. You ran into the street after a ball. Go back 2 spaces. 3. You didn't cross with the crossing guard. Go back 1 space.

EVERYTHING LEARNING GAME

YOU NEED:

- A large piece of cardboard
- Marking pens
- Markers for each player: bottle caps, small toys
- Dice or a cube with 1-6 dots

YOU DO:

1. Draw a winding sidewalk or path on the cardboard with about 100 squares, a START and a FINISH.

2. Place letters, numerals (1-10), shapes (○ △ □ ⊂⊃) along the walk. Color the shapes different colors. You could also draw simple pictures: toys, animals, flowers, fruit, holidays, etc.

3. Each player rolls the die and moves that number of spaces.

4. When he lands, he tells the number, color, shape, letter, etc. If he says it wrong, he must go back to his starting point.

5. Whoever reaches FINISH first is the winner.

To make the game harder, have the player tell another word that starts with that letter, or what the next number is; what number you add to make 5 or 10; or what number you take away to get 2 or 3 · · · think up as many variations as you can !

MORE VARIATIONS:

- make harder cubes; replace the DOTS with numbers or number words

- use a spinner, instead of the cube

- use cards with pictures, words and numbers, instead of the cube; add BONUS cards and spaces

DIAL · A · NUMBER

YOU NEED:

- A berry basket or box
- One long and one short cardboard tube
- Two small paper cups or egg carton sections
- Brads   • Cardboard • String
- Glue   • Scissors • Markers

YOU DO:

1. To make a BASE for your phone, turn a berry basket upside down.

2. Cut the short tube lengthwise and glue half of it onto the base for a CRADLE.

3. Attach an egg carton cup to each end of the long tube for the RECEIVER.

4. To make the DIAL, cut a circle of cardboard and draw 10 smaller circles on it, numbering each For a more realistic dial, cut out another circle with 10 holes and place it on top of the first circle.

5. Push a brad through the center of the dial to attach it to the base.

HOW TO USE YOUR PHONE
- Write your number on the dial.
- Practice dialing "O" or 911 for help.
- Keep important numbers like your doctor's, the pharmacy, your grandparents', in a handy place.

FAMILY MEALS

YOU NEED:
- Newspapers or magazines
- Cardboard
- Paper plates
- Food trays or boxes
- Scissors   • Crayons
- Glue

YOU DO:

1. Look through the newspapers and magazines and cut out pictures of the various foods.

2. Paste each one on a piece of cardboard. Label them and color each one, if you wish.

3. Then sort the pictures into the FOUR MAIN FOOD GROUPS: milk and dairy products, fruits and vegetables, meat and fish, bread and cereal.

4. Paste a picture and write the name of each category on a box or food tray; then MATCH the pictures to the food groups.

5. Find the foods that you'd like to eat for each meal. Then pick one or two from each food group and paste them on paper plates or pieces of cardboard.

Breakfast:
  Orange juice
  Cereal and bananas
  Toast
  Milk or cocoa

Lunch:
  Peanut butter sandwich
  Carrot + celery sticks
  Fruit drink
  Granola cookies

Dinner:
  Meatloaf or Hamburger
  Peas and potatoes
  Lettuce + tomato salad
  Pudding — Milk

SICK-IN-BED

1. Enjoy quiet playtimes, along with your medicine, and you'll feel happier and get well sooner, too!

2. A home-made BACKREST, PLAY-TABLE and paper pin-on WASTE-BASKET will help you pass the hours more comfortably.

3. A tray or shallow baking tin with sides, plastic bag or vinyl table cloth on top of the cardboard table will keep MESS to a minimum.

4. A muffin tin or cardboard cold drink holder can keep your art supplies handy.

5. Books, T.V., storytelling, singing, puppetry, paper and pencil games, etc. will help you pass the time happily.

6. Look through this book for other quiet-time activities and projects.

7. A special family picnic-type supper (in baskets or on trays) will make mealtime more fun!

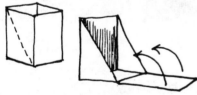

BACKREST
Cut a cardboard box on the diagonal; then fold up the flap. Tape together and cover with contact paper.

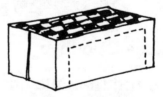

PLAY TABLE
Cut out an opening on opposite ends of a large box. Draw a checker board on the top with felt markers.

WASTEBASKET
Pin a large paper bag to the sheet, or make a holder from folded newspapers, felt or denim.

Thanks to:
Shirley & Monroe Paxmon
for these ideas.

61

Pretending

Imagination is a wonderful thing
  who do you want to be?
A ballet dancer, an astronaut or a
  sailor out at sea?

Pretend you're a green-eyed monster,
  living in a hidden cave.
Or a pirate, cowboy or police person—
  or even an Indian maid.

Pile your blocks up high for a house or a store,
  add your dolls, stuffed animals, and toys
Play dress-up with fancy grownup clothes —
  who cares about all the noise?

                          cbh

Tell the Rainy Day Blues Goodbye

There's nothing more fun than playing make-believe
  to fill up your days with joy.
All you need is to use imagination,
  along with costumes, props and a toy.
So get on your "magic carpet,"
  and sail away up in the sky.
Pretend to be anything your heart desires,
  and tell the "rainy day blues" goodbye!

                          cbh

SHADOW FUN

YOU NEED:

- A white box lid
- Crayons or markers
- Cardboard
- Scissors
- Flashlight

YOU DO:

1. Draw and cut out some simple cardboard shapes or objects.

2. Prop the box lid against something and then darken the room.

3. Next, hold a cut-out in one hand and flash your light behind it so its SHADOW appears on the white lid.

4. Try putting on a show with just your fingers (can you make a bunny or an alligator?) or by using various objects such as a stick puppet, a key, feather or leaf.

CREATE YOUR OWN
INSTANT THEATRE

1. Divide into two or more "acting teams" and write several clever "punch lines" for the other team to draw out of the "producers hat".

2. For example: "How do inch worms inch?" "Who's been eating my wheat germ?" "You mean the party was LAST Saturday?"

3. Each team plans a short impromptu play built around the punch line.

4. Some costumes and props would add to the fun... Let your imagination take over — the play is on!

JUNIOR EXECUTIVE

Set up a pretend office and make your own office equipment !

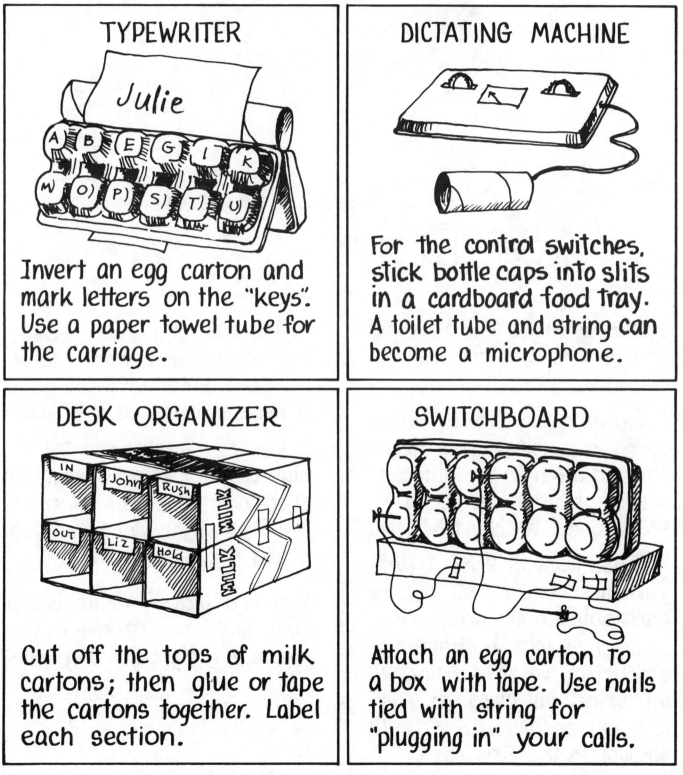

TYPEWRITER

Invert an egg carton and mark letters on the "keys". Use a paper towel tube for the carriage.

DICTATING MACHINE

For the control switches, stick bottle caps into slits in a cardboard food tray. A toilet tube and string can become a microphone.

DESK ORGANIZER

Cut off the tops of milk cartons; then glue or tape the cartons together. Label each section.

SWITCHBOARD

Attach an egg carton to a box with tape. Use nails tied with string for "plugging in" your calls.

MUSIC, MUSIC, MUSIC

1. Start by filling 2 or 3 glasses or jars with different amounts of water.

2. Tap each one GENTLY with a spoon, a pencil or your fingernail and listen to the different sounds. Which glass has a HIGH tone? Which a LOWER one?

3. If you want to PLAY A TUNE, you'll need 8 GLASSES, one for each note on the scale. Fill each glass with a different amount of water, starting with an almost full glass on your left and ending with a small amount in the 8th glass.

4. The tone of the full glass will be deep and clear. Add or pour out water until you get 8 musical notes of a SCALE.

5. Tap the glasses and try to play a tune. If you want a short note, put your finger on the rim of the glass and the sound will stop.

Can you play "Twinkle, Twinkle Little Star" or "Oh Where, Oh Where, Has My Little Dog Gone?"

MUSICAL INSTRUMENTS

1. Hammer a row of large nails into a block of wood, making them DIFFERENT heights.

2. Use another nail to scrape across them.

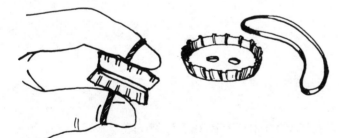

FINGER CYMBALS

1. Punch 2 holes in the center of 2 matching jar lids, large buttons or bottle caps.

2. Fold a fat rubber band in half and push each end through the holes.

3. Put your thumb and forefinger through the loops and clack away!

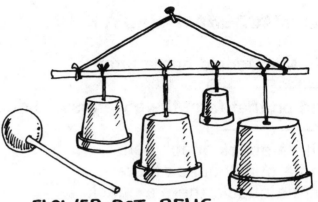

FLOWER POT BELLS

1. Hang clay flower pots, of different sizes, upside down from a wooden dowel.

2. Make a large knot at the end of a sturdy rope (or tie on a washer or curtain ring) so the rope will be secure in the pot.

3. For a STRIKER, use a dowel or pencil pushed into a rubber ball — or wrap a piece of foam rubber or styrofoam with leather or heavy fabric.

4. Attach a rope or string handle to hang the bells.

SHAKER

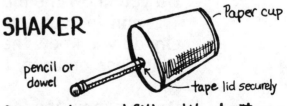

Paper cup

pencil or dowel

tape lid securely

Decorate and fill with buttons, paper clips, bottle caps, etc.

FAVORITE SONGS

OLD MACDONALD HAD A FARM

Old MacDonald had a farm
E—I—E—I—O.
And on that farm there were some ducks
E—I—E—I—O.
With a quack-quack here
And a quack-quack there.
Here a quack, there a quack
Everywhere a quack-quack.
Old MacDonald had a farm
E—I—E—I—O.

1. Sing the song the first time using ducks and the quack-quack sound that they make.
2. Each time that you sing the song *again,* use these animals:
   pig: oink-oink
   dog: bow-wow
   cow: moo-moo
   crows: caw-caw
   chickens: peep-peep
   lambs: baa-baa
   horses: neigh-neigh
   cats: meow-meow
   Think up other animals and sounds, even imaginary ones.

MUFFIN MAN

Do you know the muffin man?
The muffin man, the muffin man?
Oh, do you know the muffin man,
Who lives on Drury Lane?

Do you know the ice cream man? etc.
Do you know the pizza man? etc.

68

NICK NACK PADDY WACK

This old man, he plays "one"
  (hold up thumb)
He plays Nick Nack on his **thumb.**
  (slap thumb against other palm)

Chorus:
Nick Nack,
  (slap thumb against other palm)
Paddy Wack
  (hand against palm)
Give the dog a bone
  (Clap hands)
This old man came rolling home.
  (rotate one hand around the other)

This old man, he plays "two"
  (thumb and forefinger)
He plays Nick Nack on his **shoe.**
  (slap shoe)

Chorus:
Nick Nack, etc.

This old man, he plays "three"
  (thumb, forefinger and middle finger)
He plays Nick Nack on his **knee.**
  (slap knee)

Chorus:
Nick Nack, etc.

This old man, he plays "four"
  (next finger)
He plays Nick Nack on the **floor**
  (slap floor)

Chorus:
Nick Nack, etc.

This old man, he plays "five"
  (next finger)
He plays Nick Nack on his **eye.**
  (slap eyebrow, etc.)

Chorus:
Nick Nack, etc.

OH WHERE HAS MY LITTLE DOG GONE?

Oh where, Oh where has my little dog gone?
Oh where, oh where can he be?
With his ears cut short and his tail cut long,
Oh where, oh where can he be?

ACTION SONGS

IF YOU'RE HAPPY

If you're happy and you know it,
   Clap your hands.
If you're happy and you know it,
   Clap your hands.
If you're happy and you know it;
   Then your face will surely show it.
If you're happy and you know it,
   Clap your hands.

HOP AND JUMP

Hop on your right foot, (hop)
Hop on your left;
Jump on both feet, (jump)
That is best;
Wave with your right hand, (wave)
Wave with your left;
Nod your head and take a rest. (nod)

JUST SO

We rap, rap, rap
And we clap, clap, clap
We look to the left and then to the right.
And we nod our heads up and down
We spread or stretch our arms out wide, then high.
And we whirl all around just so.

UP AND DOWN

Up and down, up and down
Clap, clap and turn around.
Up and down, up and down,
Clap, clap, and bow.
(Reverse activities: Down, then up, etc.,
  and add various other activities.)

AN AFRICAN MOVEMENT SONG FROM GHANA

First you clap and sing,
Then you twist and sing,
Clap, clap, clap together
clap, clap away.
Clapping is an exercise,
clap, clap away.
(you could add)
Bend, bend, bend together
Bend, bend away...
or Sing, sing, sing...
Kick, kick, kick...
Hop, hop, hop...

African story tellers often wear huge hats with large brims. Hanging from the brims might be different objects such as animals. Favorite ones are the tortoise and spiders. One of the folk stories tells of how a spider came to be bald. He is like "a bad little boy who's full of mischief, does tricks, hates to work, loves to play and eat". Look up the story in the *Book of African Folk Tales,* published by Little, Brown and Co. As the story teller tells the story, all of the children act it out.

CLAP, CLAP, CLAP YOUR HANDS
(to the tune of Row, Row, Your Boat)

Clap, clap, clap your hands
Clap them now together
Clap, clap, clap your hands
Clap them now with me.

Next verses:
Nod, nod, nod your head, etc.
Stamp your feet.
Blink your eyes.
Shake your hands.
Slide your feet.
Stretch up high.

THE FINGER BAND

(Sung to "this is the way we wash our clothes")
The finger band is coming to town
   (Bring fingers from behind back, slowly, moving fingers.)
Coming to town, coming to town.
The finger band is coming to town
So early in the morning.
Here is the way we play our drums
   (Pretend to beat drums, and make sounds of drum)
Play our drums, play our drums
Here is the way we play our drums, so early in the morning.

Here is the way we blow our trumpets
   CHORUS (make appropriate motion and sound)
Here is the way we play our violins
   CHORUS (make appropriate motion and sound)
Here is the way we crash our cymbals
   (make appropriate motion and sound)
The finger band is going away
Going away, going away.
The finger band is going away,
So early in the morning.
   (Voices and sounds becoming softer)
The finger band has gone away
   (soft voices; hands returning behind back)
But they'll be back again some day.

PLAYTIME

Playtime, playtime
What are we going to do?
I'm going to jump a rope—
Won't you do it too?

Show me, show me
I can do it too.
1 - 2 - 3 - 4 - 5 - 6 - 7 - 8
8 - 7 - 6 - 5 - 4 - 3 - 2 - 1

1. Sing the song first;
   then sing and clap your hands
   to the rhythm.
2. Change the third line to:
   I'm going to play a game of tag—
   or to climb a tree—
   or to play with sand—
   to sail my boat, and so forth.

MARCHING BAND

THE DRUM

Boom boom!
  Beat imaginary drum with index
  fingers while marching.
Beat the drum!
Boom, boom! Here we come!
Boom, boom! Do not lag!
Boom, boom! Wave the flag.
  Raise right hand and wave it like a flag.

THE FLUTE

A tutor who tooted a **flute**
  Tried to teach two young tooters to toot.
Said the two to the tutor,
  "Is it harder to toot or
to tutor two tooters to toot?"

THE BIG BASS DRUM

Oh, we can play on the big bass drum,
and this is the music to it;
Boom, boom, boom goes the big bass drum
and that's the way we do it.

Oh, we can play on the triangle, etc.
(tang, tang, tang)

Oh, we can play on the castanets, etc.
(clack, clack, clack)

• Pretend to play each instrument as its name is sung.
  What others can you do?

• At the end, everyone picks a different instrument and
  marches in the band.

LET'S SING AND DANCE

HANSEL AND GRETEL

Brother Hansel,
Dance with me.
Both my hands I offer thee.
Right foot first, left foot then,
Round about and back again!

With my foot I tap, tap, tap.
With my hands I clap, clap, clap,
Right foot first, left foot then,
Round about and back again!

LOOBY LOO

Here we dance looby loo.
Here we dance looby light.
Here we dance looby loo,
All on a Saturday night.

You put your hands in.
You put your hands out.
You give your hands a shake, shake, shake
And turn yourself about.

Repeat second verse, changing the words and actions
(You put your feet in, etc.)

SKIP TO MY LOU

Skip, skip, skip to my lou,
Skip, skip, skip to my lou,
Skip, skip, skip to my lou,
Skip to my lou, my darling.

Hop, hop, hop to my lou,
Hop, hop, hop to my lou,
Hop, hop, hop to my lou,
Hop to my lou, my darling.

A POEM ABOUT MUSIC

There are songs to sing
  and bells to ring
horns to blow
  and drums to beat.

Music is everywhere; just close your eyes
  and listen.
Do you hear crisp leaves *rustling*
  in the wind,
Or a newspaper *blowing* through the air?

Or cars *honking,* a dog *barking*
  or a bird *singing* in the trees?
A frog *croaking,* crickets *chirrping*
  or clean clothes *flapping* in the breeze?

All of these *sounds* are music,
  so are bells that *ring,* clocks that *chime*
  or a sing-songy poem's *rhyme*—
Music's everywhere.

Or would you rather hear a radio, record player or cassette,
  or a song on piano, flute or guitar?
How about listening to an orchestra or a marching band?
  there's music everywhere!

cbh

INDOOR-OUTDOOR
BATTING PRACTICE

YOU NEED:

- Newspapers
- Masking tape
- Rope or string

YOU DO:

1. Crumple some newspapers into a BALL. Wind some tape around it to make it sturdy.

2. For a BAT, roll several sheets of newspaper around a long cardboard tube, then wrap with overlapping strips of tape.

3. Now the fun begins···
   Hang the ball, so that it is waist high, from a clothesline or from a rope strung between two trees.

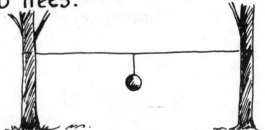

4. Whack away! The ball will keep coming back to you at the same level. Practice your batting indoors on a rainy day and you'll soon be able to use a real ball and bat outside.!

FRONT-STEP CHUTE

YOU NEED:

• A large cardboard or wooden box
• Steps, stool or low wall
• Things that roll: small cars
  or trucks, a ball, a paper
  cup, round block, spool,
  rock, marble ···
• Marker

YOU DO:

1. To make a slide, PROP UP the
   box or carton against something like
   steps, a wall, a stool, etc.

2. Then experiment by letting various objects SLIDE down
   the "chute".

3. Which things go the fastest? the slowest? Do any NOT
   MOVE at all ·· OR ·· tumble "head-over-heels". What
   happens when you make your slide steeper?

FOR VARIETY: Divide the chute into 2 lanes and
have a race with a friend!

BEAN BAG GAMES

MAKE BEAN BAGS
Cut off the end of an old mitten or sock and fill it with beans...then sew the open end shut. (Make 3 to 5 bean bags.)

MAKE A TARGET
Tape or tie together cans of various sizes, boxes, or cut-down plastic bottles. Number them, marking the higher scores on smaller containers.

Use a pail or wastebasket

Glue containers onto a board or box lid.

Cut holes in heavy cardboard. Fold in half and brace with tape.

RULES
• Players should stand behind a line and can move back one step for each turn. (Younger children should stand closer to the target.)

• Each player gets at least 3 tosses per turn and then adds his points to find his score.

FAVORITE GAMES

FOLLOW THE LEADER

Everyone lines up behind the leader and IMITATES his actions. He might skip 3 times, walk along a line on the sidewalk, hop twice, turn somersaults on the lawn, move on all fours like a dog, etc.

CIRCLE JUMP

Tie a paper bag filled with sand to a long rope. One player stands in the center of a circle. As he SWINGS THE ROPE, the others must hop over it. If a player fails to jump in time, he's "out". The last person "in" swings next.

STATUES

Everyone runs around the yard until the leader yells "FREEZE". All remain "frozen" in that position— the first to move is "out". (Variation: the leader might suggest FREEZE POSITIONS like airplanes, animals, dancers!) Take turns being the leader.

PUSSY IN THE CORNER

Each player has a home or "corner" like a tree, a magazine or square of paper, or a circle on the floor. The pussy goes from one to the other saying, "Pussy wants a corner." She is told, "Go to the next door neighbor." This continues until the players signal each other to change places. Pussy then tries to get to someone else's corner. If she succeeds, that player becomes the new pussy.

PEBBLE CHASE

1. The players line up about 20 feet from a chosen goal (such as a tree, a rock or a fence).

2. The leader walks along the line, pretending to drop a pebble (or a bottle cap) into each player's cupped hands. But she actually puts it into only **ONE** player's hand.

3. After the leader has pretended to give the pebble to all of the players, the one who has it **RUNS** for the goal. He tries not to get caught by the others, who chase him.

4. The player who receives the pebble could try to fool the others by **waiting** to run.... or **taking off** right away.

5. Whoever tags the pebble-holder first, becomes the next leader.

CATCH A FALLING STAR

YOU NEED:

- Cardboard or styrofoam food trays
- Scissors
- Paper cup
- Marking pens

YOU DO:

1. Cut a star (about 1½" diameter) from cardboard or a styrofoam food tray (or any other holiday shape).

2. Drop the star into a paper cup. Now toss it into the air and try to catch it in the cup. What happens?

3. Cut out lots of cardboard stars, adding a NUMBER on one side of each star. Toss the stars into the air and let them fall onto the floor.

4. Then TOTAL the numbers that TURN UP! Or try catching them in the cup and total the points caught. Play with one or more friends and keep score.

5. Play the same game on Valentine's Day (hearts), May Day (flowers), Halloween (pumpkins) and so on.

JUMPING ROPE

Here are four different kinds of jumpropes you can make:

- Use your knitting spool to make a long yarn rope.

- Cut plastic bread wrappers into strips and braid them.

- Wrap tape or yarn around the ends of a piece of clothesline.

- Loop rubber bands together for a "Chinese" jump rope.

There are so many ways to use a jumprope, alone or with a group.

1. Practice jumping with one foot and then the other, skipping, going backwards, hopping, turning — fast or slow.

2. Try singing this RHYME as you jump:

I can do the crisscross
I can do the kick
I can do the overall
And also the split.

3. ALL IN TOGETHER

All players BEGIN jumping together and JUMP OUT as their birth month is called. Next time, use the date (1,2,3,...) instead.

4. QUICK JUMPERS :

Oranges, oranges, big and round,
How many times can you touch the ground?

Eskimo, Eskimo, Eskimo pie,
Turn around and touch the sky.

Ice cream, soda water, gingerale and pop.
How many glasses did you drop?

Salt, mustard, vinegar, pepper !
(Turn the rope faster at "pepper".)

Handy, pandy, sugardy candy,
French almond rock.
(Repeat, doing different actions each time.)

SOME FAVORITE JUMP ROPE RHYMES
(and perhaps a few you don't know)

Jelly in the dish makes me sick
A wiggle and a woggle and a 2·4·6
Not because you're dirty
Not because you're clean
Just because you kissed a boy
  behind the magazine···
How many kisses did you get?
1- 2 -3 -4 -5 - 6 ····

My father is a butcher.
My mother wraps the meat
And I'm just a little frankfurter
Who runs along the street.

One, two, three O'Leary
Four, five, six O'Leary
Seven, eight, nine O'Leary
Ten O'Leary, the postman's here!

Donald Duck is a one-legged, one-legged, one-legged duck.
  (one-legged ··· hop on one foot)
Donald Duck is a two-legged, two-legged, two-legged duck.
  (two-legged ··· jump with both feet)
Donald Duck is a three-legged, three-legged, three-legged duck.
  (three-legged ··· touch ground with one hand)
Donald Duck is a four-legged, four-legged, four-legged duck.
  (four-legged ··· touch ground with both hands)

Teddy Bear, Teddy Bear, turn around.
Teddy Bear, Teddy Bear, touch the ground.
Teddy Bear, Teddy Bear, show your shoes.
Teddy Bear, Teddy Bear, read the news.
Teddy Bear, Teddy Bear, go upstairs.
Teddy Bear, Teddy Bear, say your prayers.
Teddy Bear, Teddy Bear turn off the light.
Teddy Bear, Teddy Bear, spell "Goodnight".
G-O-O-D-N-I-G-H-T

Charlie over the water,
Charlie over the sea,
Charlie catch a blackbird,
Can't catch me!

JUMP ROPE RHYMES

House to let,
  Apply within
When you go out
  Let_____come in.

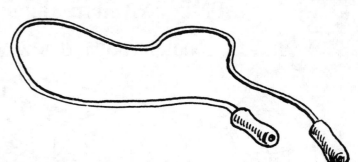

                The wind and the rain
                  and the wind blew high,
                The rain comes blattering
                  from the sky.
                (Anne Jane Murphy) says she'll die,
                If she doesn't get a fellow with
                  a rolling eye!
                              —An Irish Skipping Rope Rhyme

Eaver Weaver, chimney sweeper,
  Had a wife and couldn't keep her,
Had another, didn't love her,
  Up the chimney he did shove her.
                    —Welsh Skipping Rhyme

            I saw Esau sawing wood,
              And Esau saw I saw him;
            Though Esau saw I saw him saw,
              Still Esau went on sawing.

          Julius Caesar,
          The Roman Geezer,
            Squashed his wife
          With a lemon squeezer.
                        —Traditional English Rhymes

84

POEMS

PLAYING GAMES

Running, jumping, skipping rope
   handstands and cartwheels too.
Jacks and balls, stilts and bikes,
   All are **fun** to do.

Flying kites and gliders,
   marbles and frisbee — throw,
Hula hoops and roller skates
   help us play and grow.

Relays, hopscotch and leapfrog,
   tag and tug-of-war,
Ring toss games and shuffleboard
   who will make the highest score?

Exercise and sunshine,
   fresh air and rest times too,
Sailing boats and sandplay
   all are **good** for you!

       cbh

SECRET PLACE

Do you have a secret place
No one knows but you;
A quiet spot that's all your own?
I do!

My secret place is hidden
Beside a sparkling stream
Where tall oaks spread out friendly arms
And emerald fern fronds gleam.

In my secret place, I sit
And watch white clouds sail over;
Honeybees stop to sip
Sweet nectar from wild clover.

—*Instructor Magazine, May, 1979*

85

DO AS I SAY, NOT AS I DO

1. The players sit or stand in a circle.

2. The leader calls out an action to do, like: stand on one foot, touch your head, touch your nose, clap your hands —

3. The group must do what the leader says, but ONLY when the leader DOES exactly what he says.

4. If he calls out, "hands on your hips" but instead, he stands on one foot, the players stay still and do NOTHING.

5. When a player does the wrong thing, he must leave the circle. The last player left becomes the next leader. Which leader will trick the other players the most? How long will **you** stay in?

METRIC SHUFFLEBOARD

YOU NEED:

- A sidewalk, outdoors or a smooth surface, indoors

- A long piece of cardboard, wood or tape

- A metric ruler

- Marking pen   • Paper, 2 colors

- Margarine tubs (filled with sand)

YOU DO:

1. Using a metric ruler, mark off measurements on cardboard, wood or a long piece of tape. A good size for your board would be 30 cm. wide and 100 cm. long.

2. Mark off the measurements as shown in the illustration.

3. Cut out CIRCLES of two different colors of construction paper and paste them to the top of the margarine tub lids — three for each player. Tape lids onto tubs.

4. Players take turns shooting, trying to go PAST the opponent's tubs or to KNOCK them off.

5. Then mark down how far (in centimeters) each tub went. Who scored the highest? Can you change the centimeters into millimeters?

GET-ACQUAINTED GAMES

MY NAME IS···

1. Everyone stands in a circle. The first player begins by making some kind of GESTURE and SAYING each syllable of his name. For example, John Brownlee might clap his hands once and say "John" — then clap his hands TWICE for "Brown-lee". The other players copy him, clapping their hands and chanting his name.

2. Next, Jane Doe could tap one foot and then the other, while saying her name, "Jane Doe".

3. Debbie Smithson could touch her head and then shoulders for "Deb-bie" — then her knees and toes for "Smith-son". And, so on all around the circle.

HOWDY, PARTNER

1. Start this game with everyone holding hands in a circle.

2. When the music starts, each child grabs a partner and says, "Howdy, partner, my name is ——". Then both hop, skip, jump or run around the room together until the music stops.

3. Everyone forms a circle again. This time when the music begins, they dance or run around the room ALONE, and when it stops everyone FINDS A PARTNER and "freezes". They introduce themselves and then move around the room to more music.

4. Keep playing until everyone has met everyone else.

MOVING CREATURES

CATERPILLAR

1. Line up on your hands and knees and hold on to the ankles of the person in front of you.

2. Make a 16-LEGGED caterpillar by linking up four children.

3. Move around the room, in and out of obstacles like chairs, tables, boxes and so forth.

TRAIN

1. Hook on to each other by keeping your hands on the hips or shoulders of the person in front of you.

2. Chug around the room or yard singing a CHOO-CHOO chant.

3. Make your train go up hills SLOWLY, and down QUICKLY; stop and whistle at crossings; go backwards, forwards, etc.

SNAKE

1. First, make a 2-PEOPLE SNAKE by stretching out on your stomach and holding on to the ankles of another child.

2. Slither and slide across the floor until you meet up with ANOTHER snake. Then connect to form a 4-person snake, and so on.

3. Try to make your snake turn over, curl into a circle or go through a TUNNEL (a chair or a box with both ends open).

4. The hardest trick is to get a GROUP SNAKE to stand up!

thanks to T. Orlick for these ideas   89

ESKIMO OLYMPICS

Set up your own Eskimo Olympics by playing some of these games:

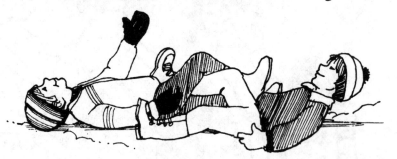

KNEEWALK – See how far you can walk on your knees, holding your feet behind you with your hands.

LEG WRESTLING – 2 players lie on a mat next to each other with heads at opposite ends, right legs touching and arms at sides. Both try to raise their right legs 2 times. On the 3rd try they **WRAP** their right legs **TOGETHER** and try to **LIFT** the other person off the mat, rolling him or her over.

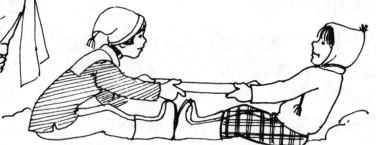

FINGER PULL – With your right hand behind your back, Lock **POINTER** fingers of your left hand with another player. At the count of 3, each tries to pull his partner over. Change hands and try again.

STICK PULL – Players sit facing each other, feet touching, and holding a foot long heavy stick or dowel between them. Each pulls to see who can hold on the longest.

ESKIMO GAMES

• SPINNING TOPS (Kaipsak)·

Each player, in turn, spins his top and then races outside the house, runs around it and tries to get back inside before the top stops spinning.

• SLEDGE GAME

6 or 7 people hitch themselves up to a dog sled and pretend they are pulling it. They must follow the directions of a driver, going left ("haw") and right ("gee") and stopping at his command. There is much barking and yelping and so forth. PRETEND you're Santa and his reindeer or Snow White and the seven dwarfs.

You can make this a summer game by using a 4-wheeled SCOOTER, WAGON or an inflatable MAT in a pool.

• MUK (the silence game)

Players sit in a circle. One person moves around the in-side and chooses someone by tapping him and calling out "MUK". That child must remain silent and NOT SMILE while the person in the middle makes funny faces and says funny things, trying to "break the muk". When he finally makes him smile or giggle, the game begins again with the "muk" in the middle.

LEAF DESIGNS

Take an Autumn walk and gather the changing leaves. When you return home, you can PRESS the colorful leaves and use them for a picture, placemat or fall decoration.

YOU NEED:

- Fall leaves
- Crayon shavings (made from scraping old crayons with scissors)
- Waxed paper
- Newspaper
- Tape
- Cardboard or styrofoam food tray
- Yarn or string
- A warm iron

YOU DO:

1. Sort the leaves according to color, size and type.

2. Press some of them between sheets of newspaper, weighted down by books (to use later.)

3. Arrange 2 or 3 of the FRESH leaves on a piece of WAXED PAPER. Use different sizes and colors.

4. Sprinkle CRAYON SHAVINGS over the leaves; then place another piece of waxed paper on top of your design.

5. An adult can help you use a WARM IRON to press the waxed paper, leaves and crayons together. ("Sandwich" the picture between sheets of newspaper before ironing.)

6. To frame your picture, cut out the inside of a FOOD TRAY, leaving a 1" border, and TAPE the leaf design to the back of the frame (trim to fit).

7. Punch holes at the top corners and tie on a piece of YARN or STRING.

8. Hang your LEAF DESIGN in front of a window and let the sunlight shine through!

SILLY NATURE HUNT

Have you ever seen a feather "growing" on a tree? Or a button hanging from a bush?

This NATURE HUNT is silly — and fun — because strange objects appear in unlikely places!

1. Hide a variety of objects in the yard or play area. Suggestions:

flowers in a sprinkling can

rubber bands on a plant

a maple leaf on a rose bush

a shell on a pine tree

2. Give the PLAYERS or TEAM LEADERS a pencil and paper for the hunt list. As they find each misplaced item, they add it to their list.

3. Tell the players to leave the objects where they find them and **NOT** to reveal the locations to the other "hunters."

4. The person or team that discovers the MOST items wins a "silly" award!

BIRDFEEDERS

Make a birdfeeder using a variety of scrap materials; then fill with bird "treats." *

1. Cut an arch in the side of a plastic BLEACH BOTTLE. Then glue it securely onto an aluminum pie tin. Let dry before hanging up.

2. Cut an opening in opposite sides of a MILK CARTON; then put a dowel across the bottom and secure with tape or glue. Attach a handle for hanging.

3. Tie a handle onto a plastic BERRY BASKET, decorate and hang from a tree branch.

4. Use a scooped-out ORANGE or GRAPEFRUIT rind with a handle of nylon thread.

5. Use a MESH BAG from potatoes or oranges to hold the treats.

6. "Stuff" a PINECONE with peanut butter and roll it in some seeds.

7. Use a leftover CORNCOB by inserting the wire ends of a coat hanger (without its tube).

8. Remove BOTH ends from a large TIN CAN, being sure there are no sharp edges. Hang up with a rope.

* Bird Treats: seeds, suet, raisins, crumbs, etc.

SHELL CRAFT

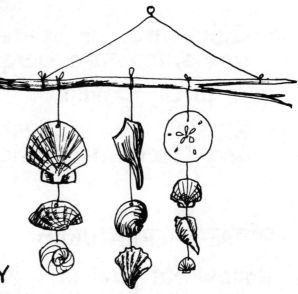

1. If you're lucky enough to live near a beach, or to visit one, you'll want to collect all kinds of shells and natural "treasures" to take home with you.

2. Rinse the shells with fresh water and scrub with an old toothbrush.

3. If you want them to have a GLOSSY finish, shine with a little mineral oil.

4. Display your favorites in a box or basket – or in a glass jar.

5. Try to IDENTIFY your shells, with the help of books from the library.

6. Use them to DECORATE a box or picture frame –wear them, too!

TO MAKE A WIND CHIME OR MOBILE:

1. You will need shells of various sizes, shapes and colors.

2. With a hammer and thin nail, CAREFULLY tap a small hole near the top of each shell. (Practice on extra shells, first.)

3. Using thread, fishing line or dental floss, make a STRING of shells. Tie each shell to keep it in place. You could add on other natural materials, such as feathers, rocks, sticks, etc.

4. Attach the strings to a stick, piece of driftwood or wooden dowel and hang on your porch, or near an open window. The "tinkling" of the shells will make a pleasant sound.

GREEN CREATURES

- Quick-growing seeds : grass, mustard, parsley, etc.
- A large potato
- Raisins, cloves, toothpicks and "face" decorations
- Potting soil
- Egg carton, margarine Tub, milk carton
- Sponges
- Marking pens

POTATO CREATURES

Hollow out part of a large potato. Use toothpicks to attach features – then add soil and seeds.

"HAIRY" CHARACTERS

Draw faces on various containers - add soil and lots of seeds for hair.

Try an egg carton DRAGON !

SPONGE SHAPES

Sprinkle a cut-out sponge with plenty of seeds. Keep moist in a saucer of water.

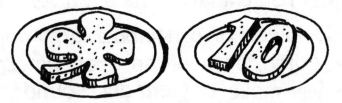

HANGING GARDENS

Poke 3 or more holes near the top of your container. Tie with string, plant the seeds and hang near a sunny window.

GROW A POTATO

YOU NEED:

- A baking potato with "eyes" and sprouts
- A clay pot, margarine tub or other container
- Potting soil

YOU DO:

1. Poke a hole in the bottom of the pot or margarine tub.

2. Line the bottom with small stones for drainage and pour in some potting soil. Bury the potato in the potting soil.

3. Place the potato plant in a sunny spot. Water a little bit every day.

4. Soon green shoots and leaves will begin pushing through the soil. Next tiny white petals will appear on your plant.

5. When the leaves turn from green to yellow, it's time to dig up your potato and see what has been happening under the soil.

6. Look at the roots and you should find three or four tiny potatoes!

TO PLANT POTATOES OUTDOORS: cut out the sprouting "eyes" from old potatoes and plant them FACE UP in the garden.

97

GROW AN AVOCADO

YOU NEED:

- A ripe avocado
- A wide mouthed jar
- 3 or 4 toothpicks
- Water

YOU DO:

1. Find a ripe avocado, and, after eating the fruit, push 3 or 4 toothpicks into the SEED and place it, pointed side up, on top of the jar opening.

2. Fill the jar with WATER so that the bottom part of the seed is covered.

3. Keep in a sunny place and add more water as needed.

4. In about 3 or 4 weeks, you will see roots growing from the bottom and a stem from the top. BE PATIENT!

5. When the root is about 3" long, your seed will be ready to be planted in a pot of soil or in the ground.

6. If you'd like a bushy plant, pinch off or PRUNE the top leaves after 4 or 5 healthy ones have grown. Keep doing this every so often.

7. To grow a TREE (it takes about 2 years to grow one 6 ft. tall!), let the plant grow 2-3 feet tall before pruning the leaves.

Note: A fat avocado seed, that has already split open, can be planted directly in a pot with soil.

BEANS & SPROUTS

YOU NEED:
- A clear glass container
- Some cotton, paper towels or a blotter
- Lima beans, kidney beans, mung or radish seeds

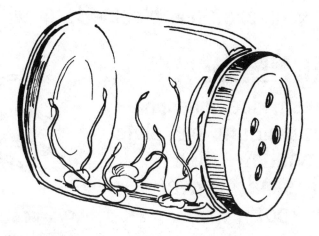

YOU DO:

1. Soak the seeds in water for at least 3 hours. Then wrap them loosely in moist paper toweling or cotton.

2. Put them inside the container near the sides. Keep warm and moist in a dark place for 2-3 days.

3. Then look and see what has happened. Are the roots growing up or down? Do you see any SPROUTS blossoming?

TO GROW SPROUTS FOR EATING

1. Place 2 tablespoons of SEEDS (sunflower, mung or soybeans, peas or lentil) in a wide-mouth jar. Cover with water and leave overnight.

2. The next day pour the water out through cheesecloth or a fine strainer. Put on the lid (with 3 or 4 holes poked in it), or cheesecloth secured with a rubber band, and place the jar ON ITS SIDE in a dark, warm place.

3. Rinse the seeds and drain off the water every morning and evening until the sprouts are ready to eat (3 to 5 days).

4. Eat the sprouts "as is" or on a salad; mix with cream cheese and spread on celery or bread for a delicious crunchy snack.

GROW A PINEAPPLE TOP

Pineapple tops are easy to grow and make beautiful houseplants. After your plant has bloomed, it will even produce baby pineapples.

YOU NEED:

- A fresh, ripe pineapple
- An aluminum pie plate or shallow dish
- Soil, sand, gravel
- Clay pot

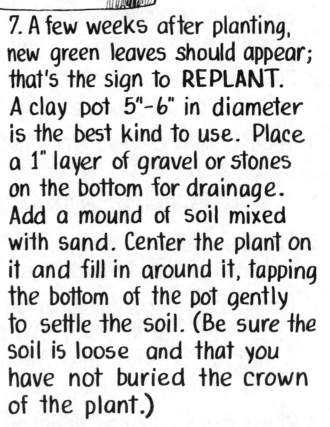

YOU DO:

1. CUT OFF the top of the pineapple, about 2" below the leaves.

2. Remove a few of the lower leaves, then let it dry for a few days before planting.

3. Start your plant in a shallow dish or container with drainage holes in the bottom.

4. Fill the container with soil, vermiculite is good, to within ½" of the rim.

5. Then PLANT the pineapple top 1" into the soil and place the container in a bright, but not sunny window.

6. Keep it just barely MOIST.

7. A few weeks after planting, new green leaves should appear; that's the sign to REPLANT. A clay pot 5"-6" in diameter is the best kind to use. Place a 1" layer of gravel or stones on the bottom for drainage. Add a mound of soil mixed with sand. Center the plant on it and fill in around it, tapping the bottom of the pot gently to settle the soil. (Be sure the soil is loose and that you have not buried the crown of the plant.)

8. Water your newly potted plant thoroughly; let drain and then water again.

PINEAPPLE TIPS

• Make sure there is good air circulation and humidity.

• A plastic bag placed loosely over the top will keep it moist until new green leaves appear.

• MIST your plant with water once or twice a day, if possible.

• A good place to put your plant is on top of the refrigerator since it gives off some heat.

• Pineapples like **BRIGHT** but not direct sun - south or west window is fine. The plant is getting enough light if leaves are shiny apple green, not deep green.

• Pineapple plants like to be outdoors in the summer.

FLOWERS and FRUIT

• Most pineapple plants live to be about 2 years of age, just after producing flowers and fruit.

• An apple will speed up the process. Just set a plastic bag over the plant with a **RIPE** apple inside and tie the bag tightly. Remove both the bag and the apple in 4-5 days.

• The flowers last only a day or so and start with a RED BUD that opens to show lavender-blue velvet petals set in a crown. Soon new leaves will form and then rows of golden yellow **FRUIT** will appear on the bottom of the new leaves.

• After the flowers and fruit appear, the pineapple plant dies, leaving little babies called SUCKERS at the base of the plant. When these are a few inches high, cut them off and pot in sand or vermiculite as you did the pineapple top.

THE GARDEN

GARDENING FACTS

1. The oldest and largest seed catalogue company in the United States is the W. Atlee Burpee Co., established in 1876. Their **1979** catalogue (that for many people is the "first sign of Spring!") featured 69 different kinds of **marigolds**, 21 varieties of **cucumbers** and 37 kinds of **tomatoes**, including miniature ones growing in pots.
2. Sugar-snap **peas,** that can be eaten right off the vine, were one of 1979's best sellers.
3. **1978's** best seller was **Butterbush Squash,** a 1½ pound vegetable growing in 3 to 4 foot vines, instead of the usual 8 to 12 foot ones. Other dwarf items were 6 to 8 pound **melons** on 3½ foot vines, midget **eggplant,** Tom Thumb **lettuce,** 2½ foot **Cantaloup(e)** plants and **cucumbers** that need only 2 square feet of soil.
4. Miniature windowsill **roses** and small **fruit** trees about 5 feet high were also popular.
5. Seed companies are constantly working on **new** varieties of fruits, flowers and vegetable for us to plant in our gardens, even if we have only a **tiny** spot available.

MY GARDEN

My garden is aglow with bright colored flowers:
crocus, snowdrops, tulips and daffodils,
grown from bulbs in the early spring,
after sleeping snugly under the ground all winter long.

Zinnias, asters, bachelor buttons,
marigolds and phlox
grow in my garden from seeds—
to brighten a long summer day.

MY GARDEN

My tomato plants are full
 of ants,
My carrots and beans
 look dreary
Bunnies ate my lettuce leaves
But at least the **weeds**
 look cheery!

ANIMALS AND INSECTS

IN WINTERTIME*

Into their hives the busy bees crawl,
Into the ant hill go ants one and all,
The brown caterpillars have hidden their heads,
They spin silk cocoons for their snug little beds.
The squirrels have gone into their holes in the tree.
The birds' nests are empty,
No birds do we see.

by JANE HUTTER

* **Resources for Creative Preschool Teaching.**
    Reprinted with permission

THE TURTLE

I have a little turtle who lives in
    some sand,
He swims down in the water, and
    crawls up on the land.
He snapped at a spider, and he
    snapped at a flea,
He snapped at a minnow, and he
    snapped at me.
He caught the spider and he caught
    the flea,
He caught the minnow, but he
    didn't catch me!

GLOWWORM

"Never talk down to a glowworm
Such as What do you knowworm?
How's it down belowworm?
Guess you're quite a slowworm.
No.   Just say
            "Hellowworm!"

David McCord
Reprinted with permission

JUMP OR JIGGLE

Frogs jump
Caterpillars hump

Worms wiggle
Bugs jiggle

Rabbits hop
Horses clop

Snakes slide
Seagulls glide

Mice creep
Deer leap

Puppies bounce
Kittens pounce

Lions stalk—
But—
I walk!

Evelyn Beyer
Instructor Magazine
Reprinted with permission

BACKYARD ZOO

INSECTS

1. Find an ANTHILL and watch the busy ant family. Can you observe workers tunneling, hauling or building? Or "scouts" searching for food and "nursemaids" helping their young?

2. Watch GRASSHOPPERS JUMP, pushing off with enormous back legs; Measure their jumps and see who can record the longest!

3. DIG up a patch of ground and spread the soil out on an old pillow case or box lid. Did you find any worms? How many other varieties of INSECTS can you count? Can you sketch them?

4. AT NIGHT... listen to the crickets "hum" and watch the fireflies "light up."

INSECT HOME

Make a TEMPORARY home for a grasshopper, butterfly, ladybug or beetle. After you've observed them closely for a day or two, turn them loose again.

screening or net

CRICKET CAGE

jar lid with water

←dirt

Hunt for CRICKETS under stones and rotting logs. Crickets like: moist bread or cornmeal; a lettuce or cabbage leaf; a piece of apple; some breakfast cereal or a dab of peanut butter.

Notice how the MALES CHIRP by **rubbing** one wing over the other!

BIRD WATCHING

BIRDBATH

A homemade birdbath will attract birds during the hot summer months. Fill a pie tin or garbage can lid with water and place in a SHADY spot off the ground... perhaps on a wall or tree stump. You might plant marigolds around your bird bath for natural seed.

BIRDWATCHING

Set out EARLY in the morning (4:00-7:00 is best), wearing drab colored clothes; and bring along a pad and pencil for note-taking and sketching. ... Binoculars add to the fun.

- Observe each bird's way of HOPPING and FLYING.

- Notice the different FEATHERS and MARKINGS.

- The SHAPE of the BEAK is a clue to the kind of food a bird eats.

- Try to learn a BIRD CALL

FEATHER COLLECTING

The best time to find feathers is from July to early September. Study them under a magnifying glass. How many can you find and identify?
What can you do with your feather collection?

MAKE A CLOCK

YOU NEED:
- Paper plate
- Cardboard
- Scissors
- Ruler & pencil
- Brad fastener
- Crayons or markers

Breakfast   Lunch

Dinner   Bedtime

YOU DO:

1. DRAW IN THE CLOCK **NUMBERS** (dividing your plate into quarters will help you place the numbers correctly.) With a ruler, lightly draw a line across the widest part of the plate; repeat, dividing the plate in half the opposite way.

2. DRAW and cut out TWO CARDBOARD **ARROWS** for hands, making one **long** for the minutes and one **short** for the hours.

3. Attach them to the center of the plate (where the two lines cross) with a brad fastener.

4. Think about what happens at **VARIOUS TIMES** of the day... breakfast - 8 o'clock, mailman comes at 10 o'clock; lunch - 12 noon; bedtime - 7:30... and MOVE THE HANDS to show this.

CLOCK GAME

Make a set of CARDS from paper or cardboard. Write a TIME on each card (6:30, 10:15, etc.) or paste magazine or newspaper pictures onto the cards to show breakfast time, school-time, Mom or Dad getting home from work, etc.

Take turns DRAWING A CARD from the pile and moving the clock hands to match it.

YESTERDAY, TODAY AND TOMORROW

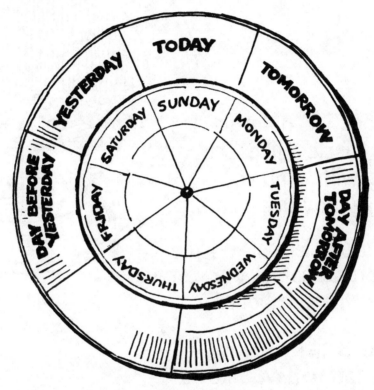

1. Divide a SMALL paper plate into 7 equal SECTIONS.

2. Print the name of each day of the week at the top of each section, starting with Sunday and going in order around the plate.

3. Divide the LARGER paper plate into 7 SECTIONS also. Write the following words in this order (the last 2 sections will be empty): DAY BEFORE YESTERDAY, YESTERDAY, TODAY, TOMORROW, DAY AFTER TOMORROW.

4. Put the two plates together with a brad fastener in the center. Turn the smaller plate to match "TODAY" to the correct day.

DIVIDING UP THE DAY

YOU DO:

1. Make a clock on a large cardboard circle (like one that comes with a pizza). Show the 12 daytime hours.

2. Then glue a smaller paper plate onto the pizza board (or draw a circle on the cardboard).

3. Now make a list of your activities for a day, like:

8:00-8:30	Wake up, wash up & get dressed		3:00- 5:00	Playtime and snack
8:30 -9:00	Time for breakfast		5:00 - 6:00	Help with dinner, watch TV, etc
9:00 -12	School		6:00 - 7:00	Dinner hour
12 - 1:00	Lunchtime		7:00 - 8:00	A bedtime story or a quiet game
1:00- 3:00	School or naptime			Lights out !

4. BLOCK OFF the sections of time from your list on the paper plate. Color each activity a different color — maybe RED for eating, GREEN for school, BLUE for playtime, etc.

5. If you wish, put pictures or words in each section.

6. Attach an arrow to the clock with a brad fastener. Using your list, point to the time period that MATCHES.

TIME YOUR DAY

TWO ACTIVITIES TO HELP UNDERSTAND HOW LONG A DAY IS

1. Think about all of the things you do during the day, from the time you get up in the morning until you go to sleep at night.

2. Dictate or write a list of them as you did on p. 108.

8:00	time to get up	4:00	TV show, playtime
8:30	breakfast	5:00	help with dinner
9:00	school bell rings	6:00	Dad comes home
12:00	lunch	6:30	dinner
1:00	back to school	7:00	playtime
3:00	school's out	8:00	to bed

3. Make a book with a page for every hour. Draw or cut out pictures that show what you do during each hour.

4. You **could** draw a clock showing the TIME on each page.

MAKE A DIGITAL CLOCK

1. Cut out a large rectangle of cardboard; OR use a long, narrow box. Then cut out 3 narrow strips of construction paper.

2. On the first strip, write the numerals 1 through 12; on the second one, the numerals 1 through 5; and on the third, the numerals 0 through 9.

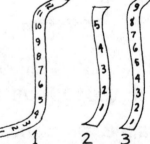

3. Draw a clock face on the left side of the rectangle, and with a brad fastener, attach 2 movable hands.

4. Cut three pairs of slits next to the clock face and push the strips through.

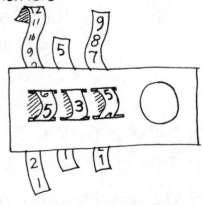

5. "Set" the clock hands, and move each strip to match the time.

EGG CARTON CALENDAR

YOU NEED:

- An egg carton
- Construction paper
- Scissors
- Paste
- Newspaper and magazine pictures

Adapted from Instructor Magazine

YOU DO:

1. Find or draw a SMALL PICTURE for each month (like a snowman for January, an umbrella for April, flowers for May, etc.). Paste one in each of the egg carton cups, starting in the upper left-hand corner with January.

2. To make "flaps" for covering each cup, cut out 12 circles or squares and write the name of a month on each one.

3. Paste or tape the top edge of the flaps over the matching cups.

4. As each month changes, TAKE OFF the flap. By December, you will see the whole year in pictures!

INDIAN MONTHS

January SNOW | February HUNGER | March CROW | April GRASS | May PLANTING | June ROSE | July THUNDER | August HARVEST | September HUNTING | October FALLING LEAF | November BEAVER | December LONG NIGHT

WEATHER WATCH

YOU NEED:
- A large piece of cardboard
- Crayons or felt markers
- Colored construction paper
- Ruler   • Scissors
- Pencil   • Glue

YOU DO:

1. Draw a CALENDAR on the cardboard. Include the month and days of the week, with a square for each date.

2. Draw and cutout SHAPES or SYMBOLS from construction paper that tell the weather:

   ☀ Sun for a bright day   ☁ clouds for an overcast day

   ☂ umbrella for a rainy day   ⛄ snowman for a snowy day

   or whatever symbol you want to use...

3. LOOK OUT THE WINDOW each morning and check the weather. Listen to the weather-cast.

4. DRAW or PASTE on the appropriate symbol for that day. Mark down the temperature too.

5. At the end of the month, COUNT the shapes. How many sunny days were there? Did it rain or snow?

   Make a NEW calendar for EACH month. Which month had the most rain? the most snow? Which was the hottest month of the year?

WEATHER PLATES

One way to learn about the new Celsius temperatures is to FEEL them.

YOU NEED:
- 4 paper plates
- Crayons or markers
- Scissors
- Scraps of material

YOU DO:
1. Pick out four temperatures, one for each season of the year.
2. Think what kind of clothing you would wear when it is VERY cold (0°C.); MODERATELY cold (10°C.); mild (20°C.) and hot (30°C.).
3. Then mark these temperatures down on 4 paper plates.
4. Draw a girl or boy on each one and "dress" her or him according to the weather on each plate.
5. What kind of weather FEELS the best to you?

WEATHER POEMS

WEATHER FORECAST

Winter weather
Sounds like this
Oo-oo-oo
Crunch—
Quiver!

Winter weather
Feels like this
Ice—
Blue—
Shiver!

Winter weather
Looks like this
Gray—
White—
Silver!

By Billie M. Phillips
Early Years Magazine

Reprinted with permission

KITE DAYS

A Kite, a sky and a good firm breeze,
  and a acre of ground away from trees.
Add one hundred yards of clean,
  strong string,
Boy, Oh boy, that means Spring!

RAIN

Rain on green grass,
And rain on the tree,
Rain on the roof top,

But not on me.

WIND AND RAIN

Where is the rain that fell last week?
Playing tag in a mountain creek;
Feeding the roots of a blossoming tree;
Visiting friends back home in the sea;
Where is the wind that blew last night?
Joining a jet-stream altitude flight;
Teaching an eaglet to wheel and soar;
Cleaning a littered, trampled shore.

—Instructor magazine, May, 1979

THE SEASONS

FALL LEAVES

I like to rake the leaves
 into a pile so high.
Then step back
 a little ways
And jump up to the sky!

WINTER GOODBYE

Winter Goodbye,
Blue is the sky.
You have been jolly fun,
But now your stay is done.
Blue is the sky,
Winter goodbye.

THE SEASONS

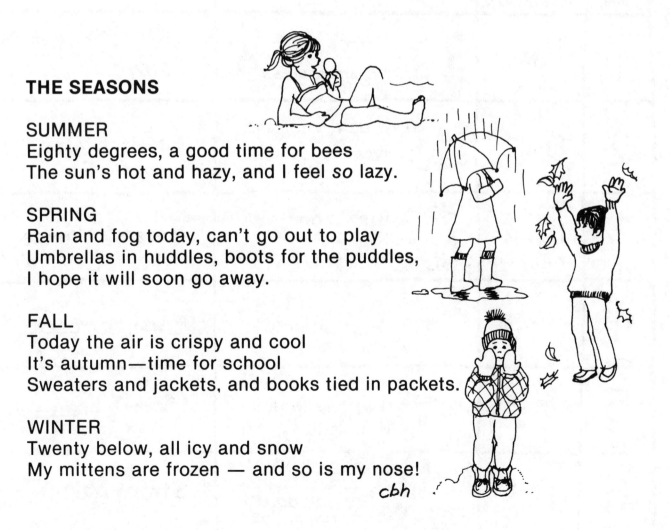

SUMMER
Eighty degrees, a good time for bees
The sun's hot and hazy, and I feel *so* lazy.

SPRING
Rain and fog today, can't go out to play
Umbrellas in huddles, boots for the puddles,
I hope it will soon go away.

FALL
Today the air is crispy and cool
It's autumn—time for school
Sweaters and jackets, and books tied in packets.

WINTER
Twenty below, all icy and snow
My mittens are frozen — and so is my nose!

cbh

CHARTING THE WIND

How can you tell whether the wind is blowing hard enough to fly your kite or sail a boat on the pond? One way to tell is by looking out of the window to see what is happening. Then use pictures or words to mark down on a chart what you observed. Weather people use something called the Beaufort Scale. This chart is a simple version; the real one used by the U.S. Weather Bureau ranges from 0 (calm) to 12 (hurricane).

MY WIND CHART

FORCE NUMBER	WIND SPEED MILES PER HOUR	WHAT YOU SEE	ACTUALLY
1	Less than 1	Flags droop... Chimney smoke goes straight up.	Calm
2	8 to 12	Good day for sailing! Leaves & twigs move.	Gentle breeze
3	13 to 18	Papers and leaves blow around.	Moderate breeze
4	19 to 25	Go fly your kite!	Fresh breeze
5	25 to 31	Hold onto your umbrella!	Strong breeze
6	47 to 54	Branches may fall down. STAY INSIDE!	Strong gale!

MAKE YOUR OWN
WEATHER VANE

Metal or wooden Weather Vanes, sitting on top of barns, churches and houses, used to be a common sight on farms and in towns of rural America.

Used for telling the DIRECTION of the wind, the vanes came in MANY FORMS; sailing ships and whales; roosters, horses and other animals; even people at work, like a blacksmith or cobbler.

Put together your own HOME-MADE WEATHER VANE:

1. Draw and cut out a large shape (rooster, boat, fish, etc.) from cardboard, styrofoam or an aluminum pie pan.

2. Glue a SPOOL onto a wood or styrofoam BASE and mark the compass points — N, E, S, W.

3. Attach a cardboard or tin arrow to a plastic DRINKING STRAW and stick it into the spool. (Be sure to use a HEAVY straw or a dowel.)

4. Tape your "shape" to the top of the straw; then place your weather vane outside where it will catch the wind.

5. Watch and see what direction the arrow points!

PAPER GLIDER

1. Fold an 8½" × 11" piece of paper in half lengthwise.

2. Open it up and fold down the two corners of one end to the crease in the center.

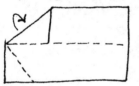

3. Then fold these corners again to the center.

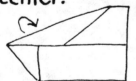

4. Bring up the sides until they meet.

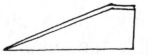

5. Leaving a little space along the bottom, fold each side down for the wings.

6. Glue or staple the nose together — the tail, too.

7. Put 2 paper clips onto the front of the wings and clip a light weight to the top of the tail (a piece of cardboard tube, a thick rubber band – or whatever you can fashion).

Hold the bottom of the glider and LAUNCH it into the wind!

PINWHEEL

YOU NEED:

- A square piece of paper
- An eraser-tipped pencil
- A small nail or pin
- Scissors • Wind

YOU DO:

1. Fold the paper diagonally, from corner to corner, twice. The fold lines should look like an X.

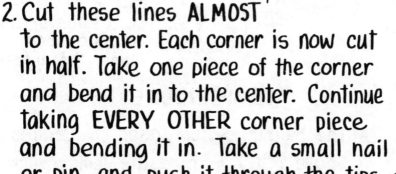

2. Cut these lines ALMOST to the center. Each corner is now cut in half. Take one piece of the corner and bend it in to the center. Continue taking EVERY OTHER corner piece and bending it in. Take a small nail or pin and push it through the tips of the pieces you have bent in.

3. Push the nail or pin into the ERASER part of your pencil. Now, run with your "Wind-Mill" in the wind and see it turn!

4. This is what happens when the wind blows against the blades of REAL windmills.

WINDMILLS

Did you know that the *largest* windmill in the world is in Boone, N. Carolina? It's huge blade is as long as two basketball courts! The energy generated from this windmill is enough to supply electricity for 50 houses.

UNDERSTANDING METRICS

LENGTH

1000 millimeters = 1 meter
100 centimeters = 1 meter
1000 meters = 1 kilometer

| 1 yard = 36 inches |
| 1 meter = 39.37 inches |

..a meter is a little more than a yard..

WEIGHT

1000 milligrams = 1 gram
100 centigrams = 1 gram
1000 grams = 1 kilogram

.. a kilogram is a little more than 2 pounds..

VOLUME

1000 milliliters = 1 liter
100 centiliters = 1 liter

.. a liter is a little more than a quart ...

.. 4 liters equal a little more than a gallon ..

TEMPERATURE

The metric system uses the Celsius scale (°C) to measure temperature.

0°C = water freezes (32°F)
10°C = a warm winter day (50°F)
20°C = a spring day (68°F)
30°C = a hot summer day (86°F)
37°C = normal body temp. (98.6°F)
40°C = a VERY hot day (104°F)
100°C = water boils (212°F)

See p. 113 for more ideas.

MAKE A CELSIUS THERMOMETER

1. Glue a large Fahrenheit thermometer to a heavy piece of cardboard (or draw one).

2. Then write in the Celsius degrees along the side of the thermometer. Start with these three temperatures:
   - 32°F = 0°C
   - 122°F = 50°C
   - 212°F = 100°C

3. Mark off 20 equal units between 0° and 200°C and write in the correct numbers (increase each one by 5).

4. Check the weather each day in the newspaper or on TV, and write it down in degrees Celsius. Soon you will learn the new temperatures by heart!

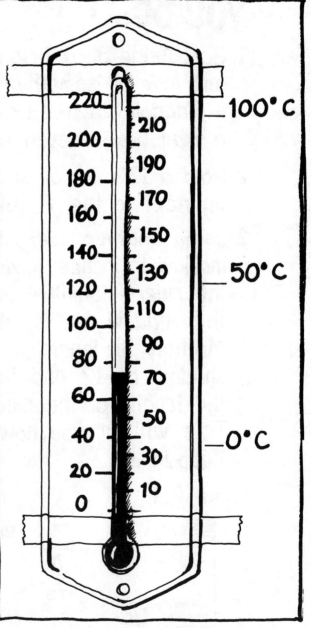

For a "ZIPPY" THERMOMETER, just staple or glue a long red zipper to a strip of cardboard. Then move the zipper up and down to match the temperature.

SHADOW MEASURING

Guess the height of an object by its shadow

YOU DO:

1. Go outside on a bright, sunny day and look for something to MEASURE: a flagpole, a tree or bush, a stop sign, a mail box, or even a person...

2. Hold a 12" ruler or stick straight up next to the FLAGPOLE.

3. Using another ruler, or a string marked in inches, measure how long the ruler's SHADOW is; then measure the shadow cast by the flagpole. Multiply the length of that shadow by 12 and then divide by the length of the ruler's shadow. This will tell you how TALL the flagpole is.

EXAMPLE:

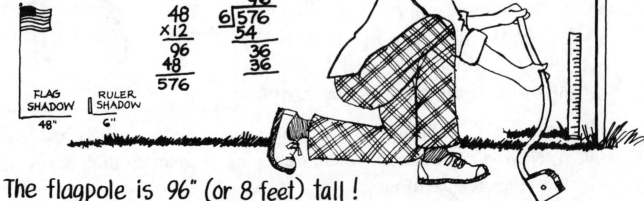

$$\begin{array}{r} 48 \\ \times 12 \\ \hline 96 \\ 48 \\ \hline 576 \end{array}$$

$$\begin{array}{r} 96" \\ 6\overline{)576} \\ 54 \\ \hline 36 \\ 36 \end{array}$$

FLAG SHADOW 48"   RULER SHADOW 6"

The flagpole is 96" (or 8 feet) tall!

SUN MEASURING

YOU NEED:

- a hot summer day
- 2 big nails
- a measuring tape or ruler

YOU DO:

1. Leave a big nail in the SUN, and another one in the SHADE.

2. Let them stay there an hour, then pick up each one. Is one nail WARMER than the other? Which one? (The reason — the sun is SO hot that its warmth can travel to warm the earth and the things that are on it. The sun warms the nail lying in the sun, but NOT the one in the shade.)

3. NEXT, stand in the sunshine and have a friend MEASURE your SHADOW. Is it longer or shorter than you are?

4. Measure your shadow at DIFFERENT TIMES during the day. When is it longest? When is it shortest?
Your shadow is LONG when the sun is low in the sky, in early morning or late afternoon. Your shadow is SHORT when the sun is high in the sky, near noon.
CAN YOU CATCH YOUR SHADOW?

WEIGHING & MEASURING

All you need is a kitchen or bathroom SCALE to have an experimental laboratory!

1. Gather up some small objects like a toy car, a block, a doll or stuffed animal.

2. First, GUESS how much each one weighs; then place it on the scale and see how close you came to the real weight.

3. It's fun to COMPARE the weights of different things: What do you think weighs more ··· an apple or a potato? key or toothbrush? an acorn or shell?

4. Do you think something LARGE is heavier than something SMALL? To find out, weigh a box of potato chips or cereal, and then a can of soup or a jar of jelly.

5. Can you get your puppy to sit still on the scale? Does it weigh more than your kitten? More than your turtle?

6. Have you learned to change ounces and pounds into grams, kilograms and milligrams? To help you think in metric terms, remember that an ordinary paper clip weighs exactly ONE GRAM.

BALANCING SCALE

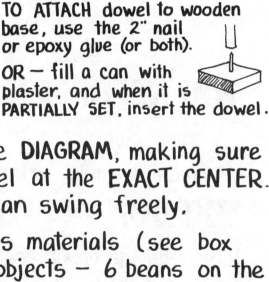

Thumb tack

Nail

Thumb tack

←—12"–14"

6"

1"

6"

YOU NEED:

- A wooden dowel or old broom handle
- Base: a block of wood OR a
       1 pound coffee can and plaster
- 2" nail or epoxy glue
- 12" wooden ruler and a 1" nail
- 2 cottage cheese or margarine tubs
- Paper clip chain or heavy string
- 2 thumb tacks

TO ATTACH dowel to wooden base, use the 2" nail or epoxy glue (or both).

OR — fill a can with plaster, and when it is PARTIALLY SET, insert the dowel.

YOU DO:

1. ASSEMBLE the parts as shown in the DIAGRAM, making sure the ruler is attached to the dowel at the EXACT CENTER. Leave ¼ inch "play" so the ruler can swing freely.

2. COMPARE THE WEIGHTS of various materials (see box below). Begin by balancing LIKE objects — 6 beans on the left = 6 beans on the right.

MATERIALS TO WEIGH:
beans, washers, dog biscuits, corks. marbles, bottle caps, nails, nuts and bolts, salt, rice, sand, etc.

WEIGHT COMPARISON:
4 nails   = _?_ marbles
4 marbles = _?_ buttons
4 buttons = _?_ beans
4 Tbs. salt = _?_ Tbs. rice

AIR EXPERIMENTS

YOU NEED:

- A paper bag

- A cream or milk carton

YOU DO:

1. Blow up the paper bag, then hit it to make it burst. What do you think happened?

2. Tape the top closed on a small milk carton. Punch a hole in the bottom. Holding it near your cheek, push in the sides. Do you feel air coming out of the hole?

3. NOW, spread out the fingers on your hand. What is between them? YOU ARE LEARNING that air is all around us. You can't see it, but it's there. The same is true of the WIND. If you look out of the window on a windy day, you will see things blowing and bending. Look for the clouds moving in the sky. Listen to the SOUNDS that the wind makes. No one can actually see the wind, but you can SEE, HEAR and FEEL what it does.

Thanks to Ilse Jacobson for this idea

WATER PROJECTS

WATER DROP MAGNIFIER

1. Cut a circle in the middle of a styrofoam food tray. Tape clear plastic wrap across the top.

2. Put a few drops of water on the plastic.

3. Look through the plastic at tiny objects such as an ant, a bug or beetle; blades of grass; a flower or weed — a coin, stamp, etc.

OIL AND WATER

Here's something to keep you spellbound for hours!

1. Fill a small jar HALF full of water and pour vegetable or mineral oil in the other half.

2. Shake in a few drops of food coloring.

3. Screw on the lid tightly and shake the jar vigorously.

4. Watch the oil and water separate to make wiggly designs.

5. Hold the jar on its side and move it gently back and forth. The designs will move more slowly now, into fascinating formations.

MAGNET GAMES

1. Did you know that a magnet attracts only things made of iron and steel? Can your fingers feel the PULL of a magnet?

2. Gather up lots of small objects and place them in a box. (Be sure to include some NOT made of metal.)—paper clips, nails, knitting needle, spool, buttons, etc.

3. See what happens when you try to LIFT objects out of the box with your magnet. Which objects work best?

4. LARGE things will attract magnets, too: fireplace tools, the refrigerator door, the base of a lamp. What else can you find that your magnet will stick to?

5. Try running a nail across the end of a magnet fifteen or twenty times, always in the same direction. See how long it takes for your "nail-magnet" to be able to pick up a pin. How long will the pin stay on the nail?

6. A magnet will also pull through PAPER, WOOD and GLASS. Try this game:
Put a paper clip in an empty glass jar. Run the magnet along the side and see the magnet "pull" the paper clip. Then add some water to the jar. What happens?

RACING COLORS

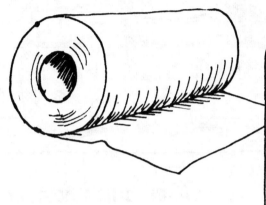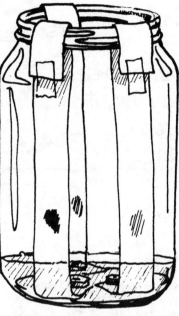

HAVE A COLOR RACE !

1. Take 3 or 4 narrow strips of paper towel or coffee filter paper, and put a dot of food coloring at the bottom of each one. (Start with "mixed colors", like orange, green and purple.)

2. Tape a weight (bobby pin, nut, bolt or paper clip) on the bottom of each strip to hold it down.

3. Suspend the strips from the top of a glass jar by taping it, or by draping it over the edge. Pour water into the jar until it covers the weights. . . . . .the race is on !

4. • What happens to the colors ?
   • Which color will run up the paper the fastest ?
   • What happens when they meet at the top ?

ANSWERS – Green will divide into yellow and blue, with yellow reaching the top first. When blue "catches up", green will appear again!

SOLAR HEAT EXPERIMENT

YOU NEED:

- 7 white plastic or paper cups
- 4 small thermometers
- Black spray paint
- Plastic wrap
- Rubber bands
- Water

YOU DO:

1. Take 3 of the cups and spray the insides black.
2. When dry, pour 2 tablespoons of water in EACH painted cup, and in ONE unpainted cup.
3. Line up the cups along a sunny window sill, as follows:
   - 1 black cup inside a white one (covered with plastic wrap & held with a rubber band).
   - 1 black cup inside a white one, UNcovered.
   - 1 white cup inside another white one, covered with plastic wrap.
   - 1 black cup, uncovered.
4. Put a small thermometer into the water in the cups.

5. After a half hour or so, look at the 4 thermometers. Which is the hottest? Which is the coolest? Can you guess why? What does the cover do?

Cup #1 was the hottest because a covered cup inside another one HOLDS THE MOST HEAT.

Cup #3 was coolest, showing that black ABSORBS sunlight while white REFLECTS it.

The cover prevents "convection" or wind loss. (Shutting doors and windows will do this, too.) Having a second cup on the outside serves as insulation, just as insulation in our house helps prevent heat loss.

COMPUTER MAGIC

YOU NEED:

- A large piece of heavy paper
- Crayons (4 colors)
- An envelope
- 3" x 5" index cards
- Glue • Paper punch
- Pencil and ruler

YOU DO:

1. Measure and draw a 3"x5" rectangle on the cardboard.

2. Divide the rectangle into 12 sections for the GRID. Color each corner square a different color.

3. Glue the envelope onto the cardboard to store your index cards.

4. Write a question on each index card, with 3 possible answers (one right and two wrong).

5. Make a colored dot next to each answer on this "computer" card. Then check the grid to see which corner has the same color as the dot next to the CORRECT answer. Punch a hole in the card at THAT corner. For example:

6. Try out the question cards on your friends. The right answer is discovered by placing the card on the grid. See what color shows through the hole!

MILK CARTON COMPUTER

YOU NEED:
- A large milk carton
- Contact paper or fluffy paint
- Index cards
- Glue or staples

YOU DO:

1. Cut a slit near the top of the milk carton.
2. Cut around 3 sides of a square (about an inch from the bottom of the carton- see illustration); then fold in the flap.
3. Open the top of the carton; then cut a strip of cardboard a little smaller than the width of the carton and a little taller than the height. Put it into the carton and tape it along the bottom and to the flap you pushed inside. This will make a **CHUTE**.
4. Close up the top of the carton and glue or staple it securely. Paint or cover carton with paper, if you wish.
5. Make your question cards slightly smaller than the slit. Write the **QUESTIONS** on the front and the **ANSWERS** on the back.
6. Now slip the card, question side up, into the computer.
7. See if your answer matches the one that comes out of the computer.!

132

BE A DETECTIVE

MAKE A MAGNIFYING GLASS TO CHECK OUT YOUR "CLUES"

YOU NEED:
- Cardboard
- Popsicle stick
- Cellophane
- Tape and glue

YOU DO:
1. Cut the inside out of 2 cardboard circles of the same size.

2. Tape or glue cellophane to one of the circles. Then tape or glue on a popsicle stick for a handle.

3. Finally, glue together the edges of the circles.

Another way to MAGNIFY your clues is to look through a jar filled with water.

CLUE

SPECIAL TRICK LENS

Use red cellophane as the lens inside your magnifying glass. Then write messages or answers to riddles with a light green marker. Scribble over it with other colors so the green writing doesn't show. When you look through your RED magnifying glass, only YOU will be able to "uncover" the messages and answers! 133

SECRET CODES

1. Use an ink pad and paper or index cards to record **FINGERPRINTS**! Keep a "file on each suspect.

Name: Frank Linden
Serial #: 1330091
Comments: Sneaky! Looks shifty eyed.

2. Use talcum powder and a paint brush to **DUST** for fingerprints. Did you know that no two fingerprints are alike?

3. Keep a little **BLACK BOOK** with your own **SECRET CODE** system.

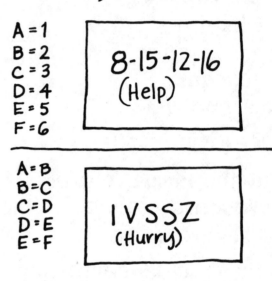

A = 1
B = 2
C = 3
D = 4
E = 5
F = 6

8-15-12-16
(Help)

A = B
B = C
C = D
D = E
E = F

I V S S Z
(Hurry)

Try using the mirror for this one!

MOT S'TI

Or, make up picture alphabets

A = ♫, B = ♛ C = ☐ E = ⊰

Can you write a rebus letter? Try and see!

INVISIBLE MESSAGES

INVISIBLE "INKS"

- orange or lemon juice
- 7-Up
- apple juice
- milk
- or 1 teaspoon sugar, salt or baking soda dissolved in 2 teaspoons of water

YOU NEED:

- sheets of paper
- small brush or Q-tip (swab)

YOU DO:

1. Write a message on a piece of paper with a small brush, a Q-tip or your finger, using any of the invisible "ink" recipes.

2. After the "ink" is completely dry, hold the paper near a hot light bulb. Not too close!

3. Watch what happens! (The writing will turn brown and you will be able to read the secret message.)

P.S. If you can't read yet, you could draw an "invisible" picture.

OTHER IDEAS

WAX PAPER MAGIC – Place some wax paper over a piece of plain paper. Write a message, pressing hard with a pencil or ball point pen.

Give the plain paper to a friend and see if he can decipher the message. The secret is to brush a "wash" of thin paint over it.

RUBBER CEMENT WRITING – Write a sentence using rubber cement. Let it dry; then brush on a thin coat of paint. Wait a few minutes. Rub off the cement and your words will appear!

SIGN LANGUAGE

People who are deaf cannot hear, but they can understand their family and friends by "reading" their lips and facial expressions, and through SIGN LANGUAGE with their hands.

Look at the illustration below and practice forming the letters. Then practice spelling out words using the letter signs. Have a friend do this too. Soon you will be able to "talk" to each other without making any sound — just FINGER SPELLING!

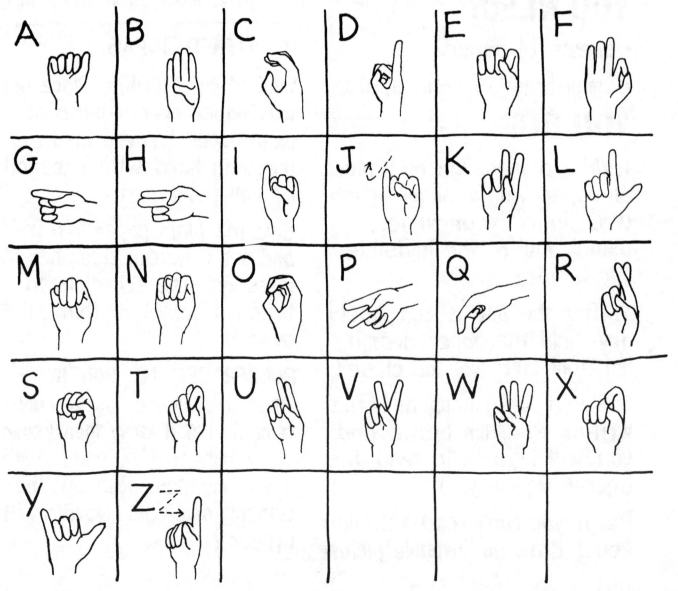

BRAILLE

What if you couldn't see at all? How could you read.? Blind people use their fingertips to read by learning the **BRAILLE ALPHABET**, a series of raised dots that stand for letters.

1. Take an index card and write your name in Braille, gluing on pieces of round cereal, crepe paper or rice for the dots. Or you could make glue "dots" and let them dry. What else could you use to improvise?

2. Can you write words or a sentence in Braille? Try and see ···

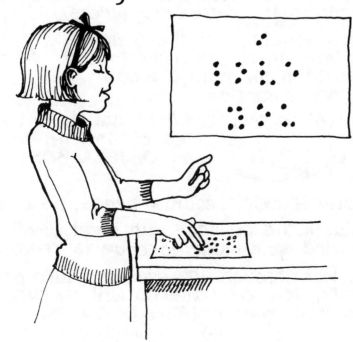

A	•	B	••
C	••	D	••
E	••	F	••
G	••	H	••
I	••	J	••
K	•	L	•
M	••	N	••
O	••	P	••
Q	••	R	••
S	••	T	••
U	••	V	••
W	••	X	••
Y	••	Z	••

KALEIDOSCOPE

YOU NEED:

- A potato chip or tennis ball can
- 2 snap-on plastic lids
- 2 mirrors or pieces of shiny Mylar plastic (approx. 1¾" x 6")
- Cardboard
- Scissors
- Ruler
- Sturdy tape
- Hammer and thick nail
- Steel wool
- Construction paper, sequins, beads, bits of beach glass

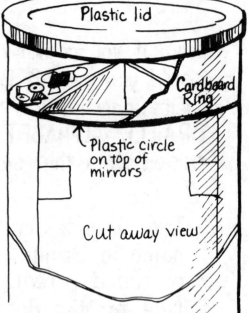

Plastic lid

Cardboard Ring

Plastic circle on top of mirrors

Cut away view

YOU DO:

1. Poke an EYE HOLE in the bottom of the can with a nail. (Enlarge it, if necessary, and tape around the edges.)

2. Cut 2 pieces of cardboard to fit inside the can, making the length ½" shorter than the can, and the width equal to one side of a triangle. — draw a triangle on the top and measure 1 side

3. Find 2 mirrors of that size or ask your hardware store to cut it for you. (You could also glue Mylar to the cardboard pieces.)

4. Tape the 2 mirrors together at the seam and then glue or tape them securely to the TOP of ONE LID (brace them with a small block of wood, if necessary.)

5. Cut out and glue a narrow band of cardboard onto the top of the lid to make an OBJECT BOX.

6. Then fill it with tiny scraps of colored paper, sequins, beads, beach glass, etc.

7. Snap the other plastic lid on top; rub steel wool across it to make it opaque and your kaleidoscope is ready.

Hold it up to the light, look through the eye hole, turn or shake the box and the dancing colored patterns will change like magic! Can you capture some with your crayons or markers?

PERISCOPE

YOU NEED:

- A tall, sturdy box
- 2 small mirrors (about 2½" x 3½")
- Cardboard strips
- Black paint or paper
- Styrofoam
- Glue • Scissors

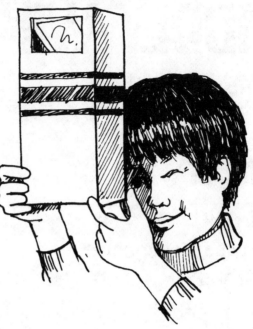

YOU DO:

1. Cut out 2 square windows (the same size as the width of the mirrors) on OPPOSITE SIDES of the box; one at the top and one at the bottom, as in the illustration.

2. Glue on cardboard strips to reinforce the sides of the box, if it isn't very strong. Paint the inside black, or glue on black paper.

3. Cover the outside of the box with contact or construction paper — or paint it with foam paint.(see page 19).

4. Cut two styrofoam triangle-shaped wedges and glue them into the corners of the box, opposite the windows. Then glue the mirrors onto the styrofoam.

5. Now, hold your periscope up and look through the bottom window.

You'll be able to see OVER things and even AROUND CORNERS!

EGG CARTON TIDDLY-WINKS

A GAME OF SKILL FOR 2 OR MORE PLAYERS

YOU NEED:

- 2 Egg cartons
- Bottle caps, poker chips, or buttons
- Marking pen
- Tape

YOU DO:

1. Fit the egg cartons inside each other and tape together.

2. Number the cups any way you wish (for scoring points).

3. Place the carton on the floor or table between the players.

4. Take turns snapping the chips into the carton. (Use one as a "jumper" and press down on the edge of it with another one to make it jump into the carton!)

5. Total up your points according to the numbers in the cups. (You might have MINUS points for landing in the lids or on the edges.) The first player to get 21 points, or whatever goal you set, is the winner!

PUZZLE PATTERNS

YOU NEED:

- Cardboard (round or rectangular)
- Crayons
- Scissors
- Pencil

YOU DO:

1. Use your pencil to divide the cardboard into sections, drawing straight, curved or zig-zaggy lines.

2. Number each section, starting with the top right hand corner.

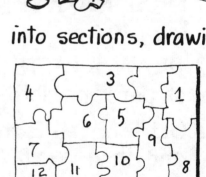

3. Then cut along the lines.

4. Turn the pieces over and make a crayon design or picture on each one.

5. Mix up the pieces and put your "patterned" puzzle" back together again. (If you get mixed up, look at the number on the back to find the correct piece.)

Variation: For a GROUP puzzle, use a large poster board and give each person ONE piece to color.

YOUR OWN TV SHOW

YOU NEED:

- A long roll of paper (or several pieces taped together)
- Crayons or markers
- Cardboard tube from paper toweling
- Glue or tape
- A medium-sized cardboard carton

YOU DO:

1. FIRST, MAKE UP A STORY...or choose a familiar folk or fairy tale.
2. DRAW or PASTE PICTURES that tell your story onto a roll of paper or cloth; the roll becomes your film.
3. GLUE or TAPE the end of the "film" to the cardboard tube and then WIND the "film" around the tube.
4. For a MOVIE SCREEN, cut a large rectangle from the BOTTOM of an open box. Make a long slit on EACH SIDE of the box to hold the film.
5. SLOWLY UNROLL the television pictures from left to right for every one to see. You might NARRATE as you go along.

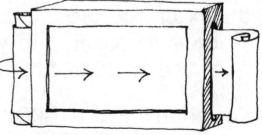

VARIATION: Older children could write captions or dialog under each picture.

PLAY PIG

YOU NEED:

- 2 dice
- A cup
- Paper
- Pencil

YOU DO:

1. To begin the game, each player rolls one of the die; the one who gets the highest number goes first. (In case of a tie, those two players roll the die again.)

2. The first player puts both dice into the cup, shakes them around and rolls them out onto the table or floor. She counts up her score and marks it down on the paper each time. She can continue rolling as long as she wishes, but if she should throw a ONE on either die, she will become a PIG and loses her score FOR THAT TURN.

3. The game continues with each person taking his turn. Anyone who rolls a "snake eyes" (two ones) gets 25 POINTS! For doubles (two threes, two fours, etc.) you get to double the points of THAT ROLL.

4. If any player reaches 100 points, it means the **last round** of the game. Everyone gets one more turn and whoever has the most points over 100 at the end is winner. Now the big question is — should you keep on throwing and make more points, or take a chance of being a PIG?

GUESSING JARS

- Clear jars with lids
- Marking pen
- Tape
- Various objects such as beans, peanuts, pennies, screws, nuts and bolts, pieces of wrapped candy, etc.

1. Line up all of the jars and have someone place different objects in each one.

2. Now guess how many there are in each jar.

3. After you have guessed, unscrew the top and pour out the contents from each jar, and count the number of pennies, nuts, beans, paper clips, etc. When you have counted the objects, write the correct number UNDER the lid. Then you can play with your friends and see how good they are at guessing.

4. Try putting the largest objects in the smallest jar, or the tiniest ones in the largest jar. Does this make it easier or harder to guess?

FLIP BOOK

YOU NEED:

- A small, thick pad of paper
- Pen, pencil, crayons or markers

YOU DO:

1. Starting with the last page of the pad of paper, draw a small, simple picture in the LOWER PART of the page. Examples: a chicken inside of an egg, a small pot with a plant growing inside, or a stick figure running.

2. On the next page (working backwards) draw the SAME picture, but this time make a change.

3. Keep drawing the SAME picture in the same spot on each page, CHANGING it slightly each time, until the the final picture is a newborn chick sitting inside of a cracked egg.

4. Now, put your thumb under the last page and FLIP the pages ... your picture will start to move, the egg will begin cracking and the chick will hatch ... just like an animated cartoon!

Thanks to Nell Minow for this idea

GUESSING GRAMMAR

This is a game to help you learn: Verbs and Adverbs

VERBS

tell you what to do, like "eat", "sing", "walk" or "smile". They are ACTION WORDS.

ADVERBS

tell you HOW to do it – "happily", "sadly", "fast", "slowly". Many of these words end in "-ly".

1. Write down some verbs and adverbs on pieces of paper and sort them into two separate piles.

2. Each player takes **ONE** word from **EACH** pile. One person acts out his two words **WITHOUT** talking. (Such as "jump noisily" or "walk happily.")

3. The first person who guesses BOTH words correctly gets to do the next pantomime!

Thanks to Nell Minow for this idea.

NEW WORDS

"It would be very funny,
If ears of the bunny
Were exchanged for the horns of the sheep.

For the sheep would then surely
Be known as the "shunny,"
And the bunny quite simply the "beep."

From <u>A Gopher in the Garden</u>
by Jack Prelutsky, MacMillan

1. This poet has made up NEW WORDS by putting two words
   together and then dropping the middle sounds and letters.

2. What do you think a shunny looks like, or a beep?

3. Can you draw a picture of a shunny?

TRY THIS GAME WITH A PARTNER:

1. Fold a long piece of paper in half, and
   on the LEFT side draw the head of
   an animal.

2. Next, fold the paper back and hand it
   to your partner, who draws an animal's
   body on the RIGHT side of the paper.

3. Open up the paper and you'll have a "new" animal.

4. Can you give it a name and make up a story about it?

ISOMETRIC EXERCISES

Stretch, bend and relax, while sitting in a chair! These isometric exercises will strengthen your muscles and make you feel better all over!

LEG STRETCHING - Sit down and tuck your feet in toward your chair. Then stretch out the left knee as far as possible while pushing your heel forward and pulling your toes in close to you. Return to the original position and relax. Repeat the same movement with the right leg. Then do BOTH legs together. Do the left, right and both leg exercises 4 times.

SHOULDER ROLLING - Move your shoulders gently and rhythmically in large circles, first forward, then backward.

IMAGINARY ROWING - Lean forward and stretch your arms out as if you were rowing a boat. Lift your feet, press down the toes, pull in your arms and at the same time lean backward, completing the stroke. Repeat for one or two minutes.

HEAD CIRCLES - Lift your chin up so you're looking at the ceiling; move your head from side to side in a circular motion. Then move it in the opposite direction. What other exercises can you do sitting down - wiggle arms, fingers, toes? Roll your eyes!

BEAUTY IS SKIN DEEP

Set up a pretend "shop" for skin care, and make these inexpensive NATURAL skin cleansers and masks for your "customers". Your Mom, aunts or older sisters will enjoy your facials.

CLEANSERS gently remove dirt that soap and water miss.

- Use Crisco or vegetable oil with a cotton ball or tissue.

- Splash on a mixture of 1 part cider vinegar and 3 parts water.

MASKS add stimulation to the skin to make it glow. Gently pat on the "recipe" you choose, being careful to keep it out of eyes and hair. Let it dry about 15 minutes. Then rinse off with warm water.

RECIPES

- Cornmeal mixed with water to make a paste mixture

- A beaten egg white

- Mixture of 2 tablespoons of milk, 1 egg, 1 teaspoon honey and 1 tablespoon wheat germ

- A mashed banana and 4 tablespoons of vegetable oil

- 1 cup of oatmeal mixed with a lightly beaten egg-white and water

- And if you live near the ocean, seaweed – for dry skin!

149

POEMS ABOUT WEAVING AND CLAY

SONG OF THE SKY LOOM

. . . .Then weave for us a garment of brightness;
May the warp be the white light of morning,
May the weft be the red light of evening,
May the fringes be falling rain,
May the border be the standing rainbow. . . .
Thus weave for us a garment of brightness
That we may walk fittingly where birds sing,
That we may walk fittingly where grass is green,
O our Mother the Earth, O our Father the Sky!

from

Songs of the Tewa
translated by Herbert Joseph Spinden
Sunstone Press, Santa Fe, New Mexico.

Reprinted with permission

WHEN CLAY SINGS

They say
the clay
remembers
the hands
that made it.

Does it
remember
the cornfields too?
And the
summer rains?
And the
ceremonies
that held
life together?

Byrd Baylor. *When Clay Sings.*
New York: Charles Scribner's Sons,
1972. Reprinted by permission of the
publisher.

STRAW AND TOOTHPICK CONSTRUCTIONS

YOU NEED:
- Toothpicks or straws
- Construction paper
- Tissue paper or cellophane
- Tempera paints • Glue
- Dried peas (soaked overnight) fun dough, corks, bits of styrofoam, marshmallows or gum drops
- Scissors • Crayons

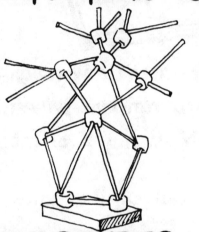

SCULPTURES
Join the straws or toothpicks together with bits of styrofoam, cork, fun dough, marshmallows, gum drops, soaked peas,etc. A small box or styrofoam box could serve as a base.

FOR OLDER CHILDREN-
Glue toothpicks together to make interesting sculptures. When thoroughly dry, paint if you wish.

STAINED GLASS SHAPES
Cut out shapes from colored cellophane or tissue paper. Lay them flat on a table and glue toothpicks around the edges. Hang or tape your stained glass design in a window.

TOOTHPICK PICTURES

Glue a design of flat toothpicks or popsicle sticks onto construction paper; then decorate your picture with crayons.

FUN WITH WOOD

YOU NEED:

- A piece of scrap wood
- Nails with large heads
- Hammer
- Sandpaper
- Paint or wood stain
- Yarn or string

YOU DO:

1. Sand a piece of wood to be sure there aren't any rough edges.

2. Pound 8 or 10 nails into the wood in a random pattern.

3. Stain the wood or paint on a DESIGN, using 2 or more colors. Let dry.

4. Then wind STRING or YARN in and out of the nails to create still another design.

OTHER IDEAS:

- Nail or glue together wood scraps of different sizes and thicknesses to create interesting shapes and "sculptures". Paint or stain them, if you wish.

- Use a hand or jig saw* to make wooden puzzles. Use as is, or glue the pieces together to make 3-D designs.

*with an adult nearby

WOOD FACTS

1. If you were to split a tree in half, this is how it would look.

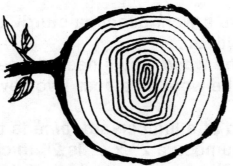

2. The outer bark protects a tree.
3. The heartwood was once the sapwood of the young tree.
4. Water goes thru the sapwood into the branches and leaves.
5. The *Cambrium layer* just inside the outer bark, is the growing part of a tree. It grows quickly during the spring months and forms *concentric rings,* one for each year.
6. If you saw across a tree trunk, you see the concentric rings.
7. When a board is cut out of a tree trunk, the growth rings form a pattern of lines and shadings called the *grain* of the wood.

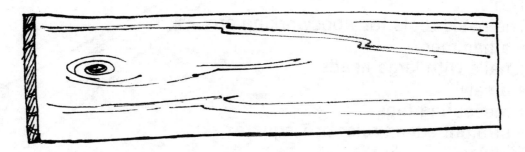

8. There are two categories of wood — softwoods (coniferous trees: pines, firs, spruces) and hardwoods (from broad-leafed trees: Maple, Oak, Walnut)
9. Knots are circular or oval irregularities in the wood.

CARPENTRY

1. You need a good place to work: a corner of your room, basement or garage.
2. If you don't have a *work bench,* a sturdy table or a large wooden packing crate will do.
3. When *sawing the wood,* you'll need a vise that clamps onto the bench to hold the wood in place. Two saw horses are the best of all!
4. If you buy wood at a lumberyard, *pine* is the easiest to cut. Ask for boards by number: a 2" x 4" is 2" thick and 4" wide; a 1" x 8" is 1" thick and 8" wide. The lumber yard will usually cut the wood the length you need. *Scraps* of wood are often free or cheap, and are perfect for making blocks and small projects.
5. Look at a piece of *wood* and you'll see a "grain", or lines that go in the *same* direction. Always sand, stain or wax wood *with* the grain, not across it. Be sure to sand your wood *before* you begin working, and afterwards too, if necessary.

6. Tools:
   The basic tools for woodworking are:
   - a hammer
   - nails with large heads
   - a saw
   - measuring tape
   - straight edged ruler or T-square
   - a vise
   - a mitre box to make straight or slanted cuts
   - a bit brace for boring holes
   - a hand drill
   - screw driver and screws
   - sandpaper
   - brushes
   - paint and stain

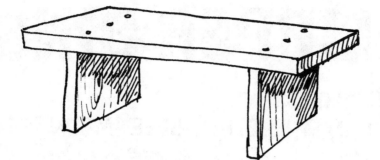

Footstool

1. Cut a 1 x 2 board, 32" long, in half.
2. Measure a line on a 1 x 8 board, 30" long, 14" from one end and cut it. You will have two boards, one *shorter* than the other.
3. Cut the short board in half for the legs.
4. Mark a line 2" from the top of each leg board and another line down the center.
5. Measure in 3" on each side of your long board and draw a line. Now place each leg board underneath and hammer in 2 or 3 nails along each line.

Bookcase with two shelves

1. Divide a 1 x 6 board, 6'8" long, into 4 parts, each 20" long. (Mark a line 20" in from the end, then 2 more lines the same distance apart.)
2. Decide how far apart you want your two shelves to be — and hammer them into the side boards.
3. Add another 20" board for a top, if you wish.

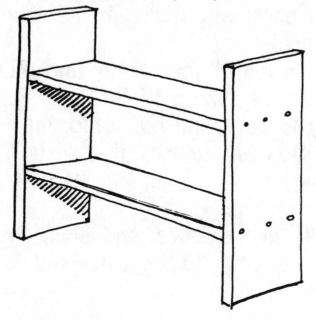

FLIPPER DINGER

AN AUTHENTIC FOLK TOY
HANDCRAFTED IN THE BLUE RIDGE MOUNTAINS

YOU NEED:

- A hollow wooden tube
  or cane about 7" long
- Plastic straw cut to 1½"
- Wooden bead (¾") or small ball
- Wire – about 10" long

YOU DO:

1. DRILL a hole in the top of the long tube about 2 inches from the end. Insert the straw and glue it in.
2. Near the same end of the long tube, attach the wire and extend it STRAIGHT UP about 3 inches. Fashion a large HOOP, bent parallel to the tube. Wind the remaining wire around the first section to REINFORCE it.
3. Push or glue a short wire through the bead or ball and bend the top into a hook.
4. Place the ball on top of the straw and BLOW gently and steadily through the tube until the ball "FLOATS" in the air.
5. As it rises, try to hook the ball onto the wire hoop. If you blow HARDER, you can unhook it, and let it float back down onto the straw.

This will take practice and skill. Probably everyone in your family will want to join you!

JACOB'S LADDER

YOU NEED:

- Smooth lath or balsa wood
- ½" wide cotton twill tape
- Glue • saw • sandpaper

YOU DO:

1. Cut EIGHT BLOCKS of the same size (2"× 3" is a about right).

2. Sand them well; then lay SEVEN of the blocks down on a flat surface.

3. Cut the tape into 21 six-inch pieces and glue them onto the blocks as shown here:
Let dry and turn over.  ←→ 3 strips on each block – one at one end, two at other end

4. Fold the tapes up and over the block; then place another block, with the tapes down, on top of the first block.

5. You will have 3 tapes sticking out. Fold these short ends UP and GLUE them onto the second block.

6. Continue stacking and gluing the tapes until you get to the 8th block on top. HOLD ONTO this TOP BLOCK by the EDGES and tip it back and forth. The other blocks will "TUMBLE" to the bottom!

PAPIER MÂCHÉ SCULPTURE

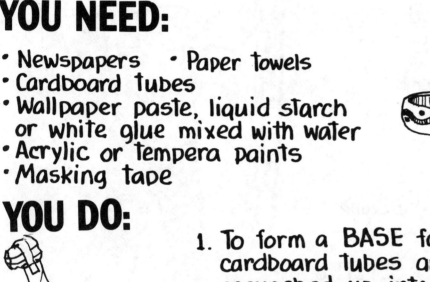

YOU NEED:

- Newspapers
- Paper towels
- Cardboard tubes
- Wallpaper paste, liquid starch or white glue mixed with water
- Acrylic or tempera paints
- Masking tape

YOU DO:

1. To form a BASE for your sculptures, use cardboard tubes and newspapers scrunched up into balls or rolled tightly and held together with masking tape. Try creating people, animals, a bowl of fruit, a tree, a ladybug, a turtle, a "monster" or any other objects or creatures you can dream up.

2. Dip STRIPS of newspaper, one at a time, into a glue mixture. (Slide the strip through your thumb and finger to remove extra liquid.)

3. Next, WRAP the strips AROUND your sculpture, smoothing the wrinkles as you go, until your object is covered with several layers. (Alternating color comics with black and white pages will help you spot missed places.)

- Using paper towelling for the last layer will make a smoother FINISH.
- Let your "creation" dry for several hours, or OVERNIGHT, before painting it. For a shiny finish, spray on shellac.

PAPIER MÂCHÉ TOTEM POLES

YOU NEED:

- Assorted cans and small boxes
- Strips of newspaper
- Wheat paste
- Cardboard
- Glue and tape
- Paint   • Shellac

YOU DO:

1. Glue 4 or 5 cans or boxes together in a high stack.

2. Cut out cardboard wings, noses, ears or other features, and tape them on.

3. Mix up wheat paste and water (see page 4). Dip newspaper strips into the mixture, and then smooth them around the cans. About 2 or 3 layers are fine.

4. Let it dry overnight. Paint with Indian designs and symbols. A coat of shellac will give it a shiny look.

NOTE: Instead of papier mâche', you can cover the cans with construction or contact paper.

SUN

MOON

STARS

RAIN CLOUDS

CLOUDS

BEANS

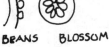
BLOSSOM

INDIAN SYMBOLS

STRIP ART

WIDE-STRIP SCULPTURE

1. Cut long narrow strips of newspaper and glue 3 or 4 together.

2. Let them dry, then paint with tempera (or leave plain).

3. Twist and bend the strips into interlocking shapes.

4. Glue your sculpture to a base (a box lid, styrofoam or wood block), holding it in place with pins until dry.

THIN-STRIP SCULPTURE

Twist 3" paste-coated strips into long ropes. Then lay them on foil and form and pinch them into various open shapes like fish, flowers, stars, animals... or anything you can dream up. When dry, paint them in bright colors. Mount your sculptures on a covered or painted box lid or styrofoam tray; secure them to a stick in a base, or hang up for a mobile.

FLOWERS

1. Cut out circles, stack them and attach to florist wire ··· or, fringe rectangles and roll together. (See illustration.)

2. Add newspaper or construction paper leaves.

3. Place in a vase (made by covering a tennis ball can or cracker box with strips of newspaper dipped in a paste mixture). Paint with tempera or acrylic, when dry.

Thanks to Instructor Magazine for these ideas.

160

POPCORN BOWL

YOU NEED:

- A large kitchen bowl
- Foil
- Newspapers
- Wallpaper paste and water
- Paint (tempera or acrylic)
- Shellac

YOU DO:

1. Cover the bowl with foil. Then layer torn newspaper strips dipped in the paste solution.

2. Smooth on three or four layers and let dry overnight.

3. Then carefully take off the paper shell and pull off the foil lining.

4. Decorate with paint. Shellac for a more permanent finish.

VARIATION: If you want to make "raised" decorations around the bowl, fold and twist long narrow strips of newspaper into a rope, dip into glue and press on top of the final paper layer.

Your friends and family will enjoy eating popcorn or other snacks out of your colorful paper bowl.

NEWSPAPER PROJECTS

NEWSPAPER MÂCHÉ CLAY

- Tear paper into small bits; soak in water and wallpaper paste. Squeeze dry through a strainer — and mold into beads (poke a toothpick through), small animals, bowls, baskets, pendants, etc. When dry, paint with tempera or acrylic paint.
- Maché clay Christmas ornaments will brighten your tree

- Fringe sheets of newspaper to decorate hats, costumes and masks. Curl the strips with scissors.
- Cover the front and back of a pulled-out coat hanger with newspaper (glue the edges). Paint and add features — glue on curled strips, or dip strips in glue and water to make hair or beards.

DINNER SETS

- Cut 2"-3" strips and weave them into a PLACEMAT. Glue the edges. Paint — then spray with shellac.

Glue strips around cardboard circles for matching napkin rings !

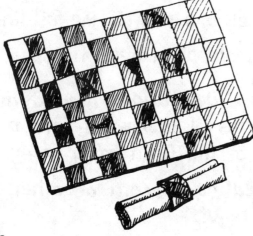

NEWSPAPER BEADS

YOU NEED:
- Sheets of newspaper
- Toothpicks
- Glue • Scissors
- Ruler • Pencil
- Darning needle
- Nylon thread or cord

YOU DO:

1. Beginning at the top of a newspaper page, mark off 1" intervals all of the way down the left hand side of the paper.
2. Then on the other side, make a mark ½" from the top. Using this mark as a starting point, mark off the rest of the side at 1" intervals.
3. Connect each left-hand mark with two opposite ones to make identical TRIANGLES.
4. Cut out the triangles and place a toothpick across the WIDE end. Wind the paper 2 or 3 times onto the toothpick, as tightly as you can.

5. Hold the paper in place and put a thin layer of GLUE along the inside of the strip. Wind your paper until the apex (point) of the triangle is securely glued.
6. REMOVE the toothpick and let the bead dry.
7. After making 10 or 12 beads, use a darning needle to thread them onto a piece of nylon thread or cord. Tie the thread ends securely and tuck the knot into one of the beads — or, tie a knot, leaving 2 long ends to make into a bow.

- COMIC STRIP beads are particularly colorful.
- You could ALTERNATE wooden beads with the paper ones for more variety.

PAPER MÂCHÉ PUPPET HEADS

YOU NEED:

- 1 C. flour, wheat or wallpaper paste

- 2 C. sawdust

- ½ C. water

this recipe should be enough for 4-5 small heads

- a pinch of salt

YOU DO:

1. Slowly mix the water with the flour or paste, salt and sawdust until it is thick enough to form into a ball.

2. Form a neck area at the bottom for attaching the clothes.

3. Then poke a hole into the neck for your finger (or insert a small cardboard tube and squeeze a little clay around it).

4. Make features for your puppet by pulling out or adding on a nose, mouth, eyes, etc.

5. Add clay hair; or glue yarn or string on later.

6. Let your puppet head dry overnight, then paint it with tempera or acrylic paints.

7. Fashion a dress or shirt out of a hankie or a square of cloth or felt.

Note: A papier-mâché mulch is also good for forming light-weight puppet heads.

PINCH-POT PEOPLE

1. For each "person," roll CLAY into 2 balls. Stick both thumbs into the middle of each ball of clay. PINCH the sides all the way around, forming a PINCH-POT.

2. Use one for the body, adding legs, arms and feet. Use the second one for the head — adding eyes, ears, nose, etc.

3. To attach the features, mix a little clay and water to make SLIP which sticks like glue. Smooth it around the features and stick the add-ons to the pots.

4. When the clay is completely dry, paint with tempera or acrylic paints and spray with shellac.

Use both the top and bottom as containers, or cover one with the other.

CUT-OUT NAMES

YOU NEED:

- Construction paper
- Crayons
- Scissors
- Glue

YOU DO:

1. Fold the paper in half lengthwise.

2. Then with a crayon, write your NAME (or a word) in script along the creased edge.

3. Cut around both sides of the crayon line, being sure that part of each letter is still on the fold.

4. Open the paper and paste the DOUBLE DESIGN onto contrasting color paper. (Put the crayon side down.)

5. Add more cut-outs and decorations to your design if you wish.

6. Exchange designs with your friends and try to guess what the hidden name or word is.

If any letter (y, g, f, j, z) goes below the line be sure to write the word ABOVE the line so only the end of the letter touches the fold.

166

Thanks to J. Romberg for these ideas.

SHADOW PICTURES

YOU NEED:

- 1 piece of (9×12) colored construction paper
- 1 smaller piece of white or light-colored paper
- 1 piece of black or dark-colored paper
- crayons or markers
- scissors
- glue

YOU DO:

1. On the white paper draw a SIMPLE picture of a person, animal or object (a house, tree, cat, car, bunny or baby ···).

2. Place the black paper underneath your drawing and, holding both together with one hand, cut around the OUTLINE.

3. Next, fold the 9"×12" piece of paper in half and glue the cut-out on the top half.

4. Glue the dark shape directly underneath the object (on the bottom half of the paper). The result is a SHADOW PICTURE. Frame the pictures for your friends.

SPINNING SNAKE

YOU NEED:

- An aluminum pie pan
- Scissors
- Marking pen
- Needle and thread
- Hammer and nail

YOU DO:

1. Cut off the sides of the pan.

2. With your marker, draw lines that look like a coiled snake.

3. Cut along the lines, leaving a small circle in the center. Poke a hole through the center with a nail and hammer.

4. Decorate your "snake" with markers or hobby paint.

5. Thread the needle and tie a BIG knot that won't slip through the center hole. Pull the thread through the hole — then hang your snake outdoors, or over a heating vent or hot radiator. Watch what happens!

6. What OTHER aluminum pans can you cut into skinny shapes? Try a rectangular one and a square one, too.

OP ART
Create an Op Art picture or placemat
from a magazine picture

YOU NEED:

- Magazines
  (or newspapers)
- Construction paper
- Clear contact paper
- Scissors
- Glue

YOU DO:

1. Cut out a brightly colored picture and fold it in half. Then cut long slits, starting at the fold and stopping about ½" from the outside edge of the picture. Try making some wavy cuts, too!

2. Now cut strips of construction paper. Unfold the picture and weave the strips in and out of the slits.

3. Trim the ends and glue them down, so they'll stay in place. Does your finished picture look slightly out of focus?

4. Make a construction paper frame for your picture, if you wish. Or cover it with clear contact paper and you can use it for a placemat!

FOIL PRINTING

YOU NEED:

- Old pieces of crayons
- A grater or potato-scraper
- An empty salt shaker with large holes
- Wax paper
- Aluminum foil
- Plain paper
- Newspapers
- An iron

YOU DO:

1. Rub the pieces of crayon across a grater. (Place a piece of wax paper underneath to catch the shavings.)

2. Pour them into an empty salt shaker and then sprinkle the bits onto some white paper on top of a pile of newspapers.

3. Cover the paper with a piece of foil.

4. Use a warm iron to press over the foil. (Ask an adult to help.)

5. Lift up the foil and put it on top of another piece of plain paper. Now iron over it again. What happens? The colors of the crayons will TRANSFER to the paper, making a print.

ROLL 'EM PRINTING

PRINT YOUR OWN WRAPPING PAPER

YOU NEED:

- A large juice can (with both ends intact) or an oatmeal or grits box
- A heavy wooden dowel, broom handle or sturdy cardboard tube
- Felt weather stripping (can be found in rolls at your hardware store) or styrofoam OR cardboard
- Rubber cement
- Variety of papers (grocery bags, shelf paper, construction paper, etc.)
- Tempera paint • Shallow pan

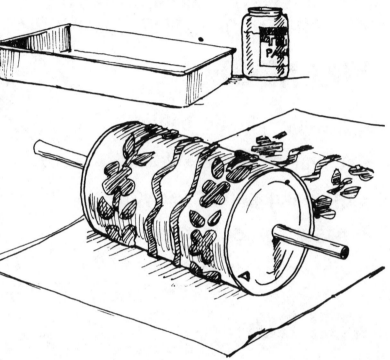

YOU DO:

1. Punch a hole in each end of the can and push the dowel through.

2. Cut out shapes from felt, foam or cardboard. You can make individual shapes or long strips.

3. Cover the sides of the can with rubber cement, and let it dry.

4. When you are ready to put the design on the can, just dab some rubber cement on the back side of the **SHAPES** and press them onto the can.

5. Pour some paint into the pan and roll the can through it.

6. As you ROLL the can over the paper, watch your design appear!

171

SCRIMSHAW

AN ANCIENT ART PRACTICED
BY SAILORS AND ESKIMOS
ON PIECES OF BONE OR IVORY

YOU NEED:

- A white plastic bottle
- A nail or large needle
- Marking pen or crayon
- Tissue or soft rag
- Ribbon or yarn

YOU DO:

1. Cut the flat parts of a plastic bottle into shapes for jewelry or a picture.
2. SCRATCH a design into the plastic with a sharp needle or nail.
3. Color over the lines with a marking pen or crayon.
4. RUB all over the plastic with a rag or tissue so that the only color left is INSIDE the scratched lines.
5. Put a hole at the top of your scrimshaw and string with ribbon or yarn for a necklace – OR – put ribbon through TWO HOLES for a bracelet.
6. For a PICTURE, glue the scrimshaw to a cardboard or construction paper frame.

172

SANDPAPER PRINTS

YOU NEED:

• Sandpaper (fine grained)
  or smooth wood

• White construction paper

• Crayons

• An iron

• Newspapers

YOU DO:

1. Pressing down hard with your crayons, draw a picture on a piece of sandpaper or wood. If using wood, make your crayon strokes go WITH the grain.

2. Then place your picture, crayon-side up on top of a pile of newspapers (on a table, desk or ironing board).

3. Lay the white paper over it and PRESS GENTLY with a WARM iron.

4. Carefully lift up the paper, and your crayon design will now be on the BACK of the white paper!

P.S. If you want any words on your picture, remember to write them backwards.

You can also make crayon prints on fabric ... draw the picture on the cloth, pressing hard with your crayons. To set the color, cover with a damp cloth and press with a hot iron. Be sure to work on a surface protected by newspapers.
Try this with a T-shirt, shorts or a placemat and napkin set.

CRAYON MOSAICS

YOU NEED:
- Bits of crayons
- A plug-in warming tray or an iron
- Foil or waxed paper
- Cardboard
- Glue
- Tempera paint

YOU DO:

1. Melt several crayons of different colors by ironing them between sheets of waxed paper, or placing them on foil on a warming tray.

2. When cool and hard, peel off the crayon blobs and break them into tiny pieces.

3. Glue the pieces onto cardboard in a design, like a mosaic.

4. Let dry and paint over the mosaic sections with tempera paint thinned with water; then use another color to paint a background.

5. What else can you do with the crayon bits?

MAGIC BATIK PAINTINGS

YOU NEED:

- Three colors of watercolor or thin tempera paint
- Paint brush
- Rubber cement & brush
- White paper

YOU DO:

1. Choose THREE colors of watercolor or thin tempera paint; for example, light yellow, medium orange and dark blue.

2. Brush over your paper with the LIGHTEST color (yellow) and let dry completely; then "paint" on a design with the RUBBER CEMENT.

3. After it dries, go over the picture with a second color of paint (orange). The parts covered with rubber cement will stay yellow.

4. Now paint additional parts of the design with more rubber cement and wash over it again, this time with the darkest color paint (blue).

5. Finally, carefully rub or pull off the rubber cement. You will be delighted with your 3-color batik painting.

WEAVING WITH STRAWS

Make yourself a belt, a guitar strap or a handle for a tote bag.

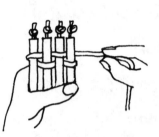

YOU NEED:
- 2 or 3 plastic drinking straws, cut in half
- Thick yarn or string

YOU DO:

1. Cut a length of yarn for each half-straw, about 20" longer than your belt will be.

2. Thread each piece through a straw (try "sucking" it through). Make a LARGE KNOT or tape the yarn to the end of the straw. Tie all the long ends together loosely near the bottom.

3. Hold the straws flat in one hand. Attach the weaving yarn to one of the straws and start to weave over and under the straws, working UP on each new row.

4. When you have woven several rows (not too tightly!), push the finished part DOWN a little way so you have room for the new rows.

5. Tie in a new piece of yarn whenever necessary, "hiding" the knot ends in your weaving.

6. You are finished when the weaving covers the area from the bottom of the straws to the loose knot. Cut the knots and slip the straws off the yarn. Tie the loose ends together and ··· you have a woven belt, strap or handle !

SPOOL KNITTING

YOU NEED:

- A large empty spool or wooden curtain ring
- 4 or 5 finishing nails (small heads)
- A crochet hook or small knitting needle
- A ball of yarn

YOU DO:

1. Pound the nails, evenly spaced, into the top of the spool or curtain ring.

2. Push the end of the yarn through the center, so the "tail" hangs from the bottom.

3. Make a LOOP of yarn around EACH nail. Then, continuing in the same direction, wind the yarn above the loop.

4. With a hook or needle, lift the bottom yarn over the top one and then OFF of the nail. Keep on working around the spool and pull down the yarn tail. Soon a knitted "rope" will appear from the bottom of the spool.

5. When your rope is long enough, use it for hanging plants, sewing into a mat, making a belt or even a jumprope!

BURLAP DESIGNS

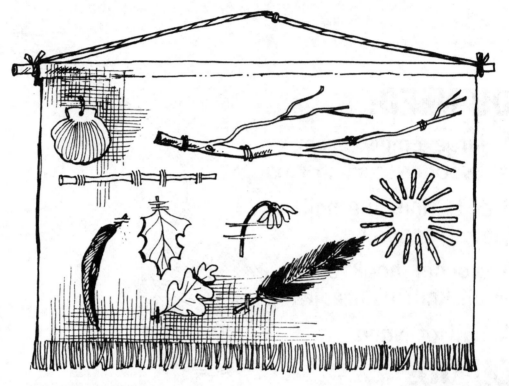

1. Cut a piece of burlap to the size you want for a wallhanging.

2. Turn the top edge back about an inch and sew across the edge to form a **hem.** Slide a dowel or curtain rod through and tie on a piece of yarn or ribbon for hanging.

3. WEAVE pieces of yarn, string, feathers, long twigs, etc., in and out of the burlap. You can also TIE in twigs, shells (with a hole in them), buttons, or whatever you have on hand, to make an interesting design.

4. PAINT A PICTURE IN YARN — With a piece of chalk, draw a SIMPLE picture on your burlap. Then with yarn scraps and a big, blunt needle, STITCH your design.

178

WEAVING ON CARDBOARD

YOU NEED:

- A stiff piece of cardboard (no bigger than 8" x 10")
- Yarn and string
- Darning needle
- Scissors

YOU DO:

1. Cut notches, ½" apart, across the top and bottom of a sheet of stiff cardboard. Weaving is a slow process, so the smaller your loom, the sooner you'll be done.

2. Wind the **WARP** string around the cardboard notches and tie off the ends, as shown in the diagram.

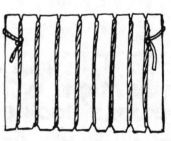

3. Thread your needle with a long piece of weaving yarn and work OVER and UNDER across the row of warp threads. As you finish each row, push the woven thread close to the finished rows ahead of it.

4. When the loom is filled, bend the cardboard to release the warp threads and remove the weaving.

REMEMBER: Your loom can be ANY SHAPE. For an irregular shape, it will help to draw parallel warp lines before cutting the notches. Round looms must have an ODD number of notches.

COOKIE CUTTER MOBILE

Hang several cookie cutters (or funnels, measuring cups, spoons, or other small kitchen items) from a wire coat hanger.

FOR THE HOLIDAYS you might want to choose cookie cutters or other objects to fit the particular holiday theme, such as hearts, pumpkins, paper snow- flakes, etc.

SOME OTHER IDEAS FOR MAKING MOBILES:

- **PEOPLE** - Decorate wooden clothespins or toilet tissue tubes to look like people; use yarn, cotton, paper etc.

- **ANIMALS** - Use a small paper plate for the body. Glue on construction paper head, ears, feet, feathers or other features.

- **BOATS** - Put a dab of clay in an empty walnut shell or bottle cap. Cut out paper sails - poke a tooth- pick through & stick it into the clay.

HOLIDAY SHAPES

YOU NEED:

- Newspapers, tissue or construction paper

- Scissors
- Stapler
- Markers

- Glue
- Paint
- Yarn

YOU DO:

1. Cut two identical shapes (pumpkin, shamrock, heart, etc.) from newspaper, tissue paper or construction paper.

2. Staple them together around the edges, leaving a space on top for stuffing with crumpled newspaper or tissue paper scraps.

3. When your shape is as fat as you want it to be, close up the opening. Decorate your creations with paint or markers and/or glue on other paper or yarn decorations.

4. When dry, hang your stuffed mobile in a window or from the ceiling.

NOTE:
Tissue paper mobiles look particularly colorful with the sun shining through them. A touch of glitter will make your shapes SPARKLE.

NEW YEAR'S GAMES

THE HIDDEN CARD

1. Everyone sits in a circle with eyes closed. The player who is "IT" hides a greeting card or a cardboard symbol (a tree, menorah, snowman, New Year's baby, etc.) somewhere in the room.

2. As each person finds the card, he quickly sits back down in the circle, not telling anyone where he spotted the card.

3. The game is over when the last person returns to the circle.

4. The first player then becomes "IT" for the next hunt.

CALENDAR TOSS

Place a LARGE CALENDAR on the floor; take turns tossing buttons, bottle caps, stones or pennies and see who can "land" CLOSEST to New Year's Day (Jan. 1) or Martin Luther King Day (Jan. 15).

Martin Luther King Day Jan. 15th ★

JANUARY

Play this game THROUGHOUT THE YEAR, aiming for someone's birth date or a holiday, such as Memorial Day in May, Father's Day in June or the 4th of July.

GROUND-HOG DAY

Friendly little ground-hog
peeping out of your hole,
Looking for your shadow up above.
Friendly little ground-hog,
What news do you bring?
Oh, please quickly tell us,
When will we have Spring?

cbh

SHADOW POEM (Groundhog Day)

Two tiny groundhogs,
Blinking beady eyes,
Decide that they will take a peek
At snowy winter skies.

One tiny groundhog,
Hearing cold winds blow,
Decides that he will stay inside
And let his sister go.

One sister groundhog,
Seeing all the ice,
Decides to wait for warmer days
To stay inside is nice!

Two tiny groundhogs,
Forgetting all their cares,
Decide that if a shadow's seen
It won't be one of theirs.

By Billie M. Phillips
Early Years Magazine

183

VALENTINE NOTEPAPER

Plan ahead and SURPRISE a special friend or relative with a gift of note paper.

1. Choose 4-6 plain sheets of paper and envelopes to make up each gift packet.

2. Deorate the paper with fabric or paper cut-outs.. (This is a good way to use up leftover scraps of cloth or wrapping paper.)

3. Make a stencil or "stamper" for coloring or printing a design.

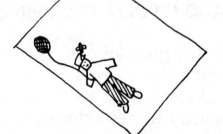

4. You could also draw a picture with a felt marker or crayon; then complete with cloth or paper cut-outs for texture.

5. Paste a matching design on each envelope. When you're all finished, wrap the packet in plastic and tie together with bright pink or red yarn.

VALENTINE PARTY

Ask everyone to come dressed in paper costumes (trimmed with hearts, of course).

1. At the party, have each guest make his or her own **PAPER CROWN**! Provide paper hearts, stickers or cut-outs to glue onto a wide band of construction paper.

2. Make a **CASTLE CENTERPIECE**! Cover a cluster of boxes with construction or tissue paper or foil, and trim with hearts, doilies, crepe paper, etc. Add watchtowers made from cardboard tubes and top with paper banners!

3. For **REFRESHMENTS**, serve ♡ shaped cookies or tarts filled with jam. Raspberry sherbet, ginger ale and fruit juice will make a sparkly punch.

To make a **SERVING TRAY**, cover a box lid with foil; trim with Valentine shapes and crepe paper ruffles; then attach a ribbon for around your neck.

EASTER EGGS

If you blow out the insides of your eggs, you can save the decorated shells for years to come — and eat the contents too!

1. Make a small hole in each end of an egg with a needle or skewer.

2. Gently blow through one end, letting the insides of the egg fall into a bowl.

3. Wash and dry the egg shell before dying or coloring it.

4. To make EGG TULIPS or NESTS FOR CHICKENS, soak the shells in water, then use a sharp scissors (a manicure one works well) to cut the shell in half in a zig-zag line.

5. A pipecleaner or lollipop stick will make a nice stem.

6. Color the shell flowers and arrange them in a decorated can or basket.

EGG TREE

Hang your colorful eggs from a branch — put a chunk of styrofoam or some clay in a painted can to hold the tree.

Paint the can or decorate it with yarn designs

To hang the Easter eggs, glue a tiny bead or small loop on top and string some thread or fishing line through.

Wrap and store your eggs for next Easter.

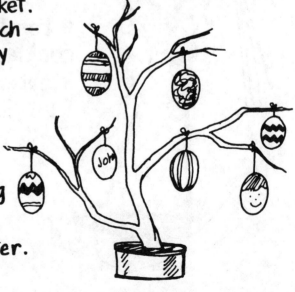

DYEING EGGS

Dye your eggs the NATURAL WAY!

When COOKING eggs, add some onion skins and you'll end up with hardboiled eggs that are various shades of yellow and tan.

Soak hardboiled eggs in pickled beet juice to make them pink —

grape juice for lavender —

and green crepe paper and water, for a light green.

Can you find some other materials to make natural dyes? Flower petals, weeds, grasses, leaves ... fruits or vegetables, too ...

Use an egg carton to hold your eggs until they are dry. Then arrange them in a bowl or basket, lined with grass or tissue paper, for an Easter decoration.

187

EASTER BASKETS

LACY STRING EGG-SHAPES:

1. Blow up a balloon; then wind several layers of THREAD or STRING around it.

2. Boil 2 cups of sugar in one cup of water; let cool, then roll the balloon in the SYRUP.

3. Hang the balloon up to dry over a sink, or an area protected with newspapers. Blot the bottom with paper towels.

4. When the string is dry, pop the balloon, cut across the top for a basket shape and remove the balloon.

5. Add a handle and decorations.

BERRY BASKET: Weave ribbon or strips of construction paper in and out of a berry basket. Add a handle and decorate with cut-out flowers, bows, buttons, etc.

PAPER BASKET: Fold a square of paper in half 4 times. Cut a slit in each corner. Fold sides up and glue each corner. Add a paper handle and decorations.

SURPRISE SANDPAIL:

Use a plastic sandpail as your "basket" and fill with grass, Easter eggs and special surprises. Tie on the shovel, too, for summertime sand fun!

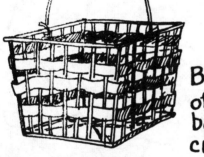

EASTER SURPRISES

Line a basket with Easter "grass" from the store; or make your own from strips of green tissue paper, crepe paper or waxed paper.

Instead of the usual CANDY, fill the basket with:
- colored hard-cooked eggs;
- peanuts, raisins, nuts, dried fruits;
- carob candies;
- an apple or an orange;
- COCONUT EGGS or RABBIT COOKIES!

Coconut Eggs:
Roll pitted dates, stuffed with almonds, in shredded coconut.

Rabbit Cookies:
1. Cut slices of whole-grain bread into bunny SHAPES with a cookie cutter or cardboard pattern.
2. Dip each one into a saucer of milk; then into some shredded coconut.
3. Place the shapes on a greased cookie sheet and bake at 400° until light brown.

SMALL SURPRISES, like a fuzzy bunny or chicken, crayons and a pad of paper, a tiny book, finger puppets, modeling clay, etc., will make the basket extra-special!

HALLOWEEN

JACK-O-LANTERN

Jack-O-Lantern, Jack-O-Lantern,
  you are such a funny sight,
As you sit there in the window
  looking out at the night.

You were once a yellow Pumpkin
  growing on a sturdy vine;
Now you are a **Jack-O-Lantern**
  see the candlelight shine!

GHOST-TIME

Put on a scarey mask
  and yell out, BOO!
Do you think the witches
  and the goblins will know that it's **you?**

MAKE A SCARECROW

CENTERPIECE

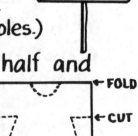

YOU NEED:

- Small paper plate or pie pan
- Cardboard tube from wire hanger
- Long tube from paper towels
- Felt, paper or cloth
- Hay, raffia or strips of crepe paper
- Styrofoam or fun dough (for base)
- Newspapers
- Glue
- Tape
- Scissors
- Stapler
- Crayons or markers

YOU DO:

1. Push the tube from a wire hanger through the paper towel tube. (Ask someone to help poke holes.)

2. Fold a large piece of felt, paper or cloth in half and sketch in CUTTING LINES. Cut out shirt.

←FOLD
←CUT

3. Spread some GLUE along the top of the horizontal tube (shoulders) and place the shirt over it.

4. STAPLE or GLUE the sides of the shirt together, then STUFF with newspaper.

5. DRAW a FACE on the plate or pie pan, then tape it onto the upright stick.

6. Add hair and DECORATIONS made of hay, raffia or crepe paper strips. Set SCARECROW in styrofoam or clay base.

7. You could also put a GIANT scarecrow in your garden to scare away unwanted "visitors" who like to eat your seeds and plants.

191

HALLOWEEN GAMES

WITCH SEAT?

1. Everyone sits in a circle, with one player sitting in the center, wearing a black witch's hat.

2. The witch cries out, "I'm a witch looking for a seat. When I call your name, Get to your feet." She then calls out two names and those people must CHANGE PLACES. If the witch gets there first, the person left out becomes the witch and puts on the black hat.

WITCHY RELAYS

1. Line up for a relay, with the first person in each line pretending to be a Halloween character: a cat, a witch, a goblin or whatever.

2. Everyone else in his line must do exactly the SAME MOTIONS or actions, as they run to the goal line and back.

3. Keep playing this over and over until each person has had a chance to be leader.

Who will get back home first? A cat padding on four feet, witch on a broomstick, or a floating ghost?

HALLOWEEN FUN

PLAN TO SCARE EVERYONE AT YOUR HALLOWEEN PARTY

1. Darken the room and make eerie sounds by cackling, screeching or clanging metal objects together.

2. Make a tunnel by lining up large open boxes or tables draped with old sheets. Tape a skeleton, bat. spider and other spooky cut-outs to the sheets and shine a flashlight to cast scary shadows in the tunnel.

3. Put each victim's hand into bowls filled with things that feel slippery or slimy (like cooked noodles. cut up Jello, olives, wet pebbles, pumpkin seeds) or whatever ghoulish things you can dream up.

THANKSGIVING TURKEYS

Here are six ideas for making Thanksgiving turkeys to use as centerpieces, place cards or decorations.

1. Paper plate and fringed tail

2. Balloon gobbler with colorful paper feathers

3. Pineapple centerpiece

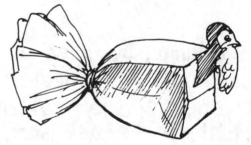

4. Brown paper bag

5. Pinecone with a fan tail

6. Papier mâché

HASTY PUDDING

You'll have a great time experimenting with this original Colonial recipe, written in old time spelling; but best of all, you can eat the results!

Take 3 pintes of new milke and 1 pinte of creame, and boyle it with a flake or 2 of mace and some nutmegg.

Put in wheat and keepe it boyling and stirring. Thicken it with eggs well beaten or wheat flower.

Put in some raysons of the sun beeing before plumpt, and streyne in some saffron, if you please, and sweeten it well with sugar, and soe serve it up.

Early Years magazine
Reprinted with permission.

CHANUKAH MENORAH

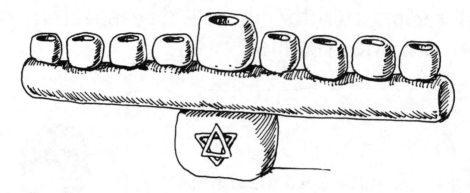

1. To make a festive menorah or candle holder, roll some clay dough into several balls.

2. You'll need a large ball, flattened at the top for the BASE.

3. Roll out a long, fat shape for the cross-bar on which the eight small candle holders sit.

4. Then make the candle holders out of small balls of clay, poking a hole in each one for the candles.

5. Finally, form a larger candle holder for the SHAMUS or "servant" candle that is used to light all of the others.

6. Attach all of the clay pieces by wetting each one before PRESSING GENTLY into place.

7. To decorate your menorah with a star shape, make two TRIANGLES from thin clay ropes, —— or wait until the clay has hardened, then paint it with tempera or acrylic paints.

8. On the first night of Chanukah, light one candle; then one more each night (starting from the right hand side) until all eight and the shamus are burning brightly!

CHANUKAH DREIDELS

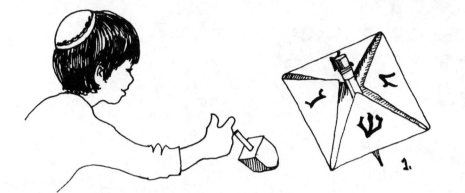

4 WAYS TO MAKE A DREIDEL
(a spinning top)

1. Put a dot in the center of a 4" square of CONSTRUCTION PAPER; then fold each corner in to the dot. Push a round toothpick or small pencil through the center.

2. Poke an orange stick, pencil or pointed dowel through a small BOX or styrofoam CUBE.

3. Form one out of CLAY; then insert a stick on top for a handle. Let dry and decorate with bright acrylic paints.

4. Using a penknife, carefully whittle a block of SOFT BALSA WOOD. Insert a sharp dowel through the center.

Whatever kind of dreidel you choose, be sure to put the 4 Hebrew letters on each side. They stand for "A great miracle happened there" (when the oil in the Temple burned for eight days).

- Now play a game by spinning your tops to see which one will spin the longest. Who can guess what letter will land on top the most times?

- Award prizes of Chanukah "gelt" (coins or small presents) to the lucky winners!

MAKE A
MATZO
BAG

(a gift to save for

PASSOVER)

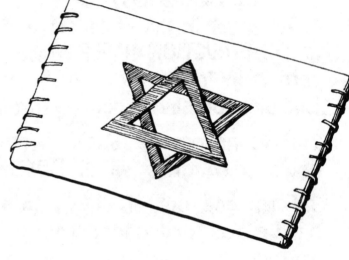

YOU NEED:

• A blue and a white piece of 9˝×12˝ felt

• Yarn

• Needle with a large eye

• Pins   • Glue   • Scissors

YOU DO:

1. Fold either the white or blue piece of felt in half and pin two sides together, leaving the top side open. Then, using the WHIP STITCH, (see illustration), sew the two sides.

2. Cut out two triangles from the other piece of felt and glue one on top of the other to make a six-pointed star.

3. Place a piece of matzos in the bag for your Passover table; or give it to a friend.

CHANUKAH COOKIES

1. Use your favorite sugar cookie mix or recipe.

2. Roll out the dough on a floured board; then lay cardboard patterns or cookie cutters on top and cut the dough into Chanukah shapes like these:

6-pointed star   dreidel   menorah   coin   candle

3. Bake according to recipe directions.

4. When cool, decorate with blue and white frosting.

   FROSTING RECIPE:
   - Mix — 2 cups of confectioners sugar
           2-3 tablespoons of water
   until it is the right thickness.
   - Put HALF of the frosting into a separate bowl and add a little bit of blue food coloring.

STAND-UP TREES

THEME TREE — some ideas for decorating a tree with a "theme" would be:
- animals • birds • flowers
- children of other lands
- fruits and vegetables
- musical instruments

Or you can cut out stars, snowflakes, paper chains— zodiac signs or snapshots to hang on your tree.

OTHER KINDS OF TREES

- A tree branch set in a can filled with Plaster of Paris; then painted and decorated.

1. Cut 2 trees, the same shape, out of heavy poster board or corrugated cardboard.

2. Make a long slit to the center of each tree; one from the top, the other from the bottom.

3. Slide the trees together, so they will stand up. Glue or tape your tree onto a cardboard stand, if you wish.

4. Paint it green (or any color you want); then **glue** Christmas decorations **onto** the branches, and an angel or star on top.

- or one made with wooden dowels.
- What other kinds of trees and decorations can you think up?

PAPER TREES

Fold a **SQUARE** of construction paper diagonally in half; then fold in half again.

With the **CENTER POINT** at the top, cut one folded edge and then the other, alternating sides (not quite all the way across).

Open the folds carefully ··· and hang from a thread through the center top.

Watch your tree take shape!

Cut a piece of construction paper into a triangle shape. Then cut this triangle into horizontal strips. **GLUE** the strips down onto a piece of paper of a contrasting color — leaving **SPACES** between the strips for a Christmas tree shape. Add a trunk at the bottom and a star on the top. Decorate with tiny beads, sequins, seeds, popcorn, and so forth.

PAPER LANTERNS

1.Cut 2 circles of THIN PAPER for each lantern, about the size of a large plate.

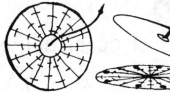

2. Fold each in half 8 times, and make 4-5 long cuts, as shown.

3.Open each circle flat and glue 1"-2" circles of HEAVY PAPER in the center. Attach thread through the middle of one of the centers.

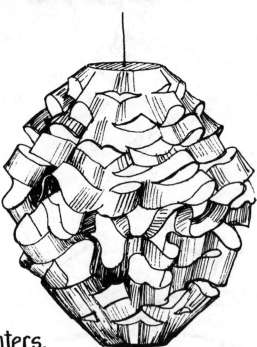

4.Put a spot of GLUE on every other FOLD of one of the flat circles. Press the other circle onto it.

5.When the glue is dry, gently pull the two circles apart and you'll have a beautiful lantern to hang up!

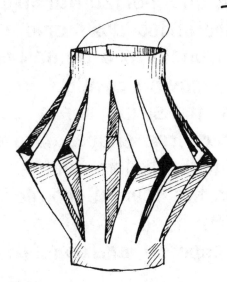

1. Start with a rectangular sheet of CONSTRUCTION PAPER. Fold in half lengthwise and make EVEN CUTS from the folded side to about 1" from the edge.

2.Open up the paper and curve the long edges into a circle. GLUE the top and bottom edges, and add a thread or paper handle for hanging.

SHRINK UPS

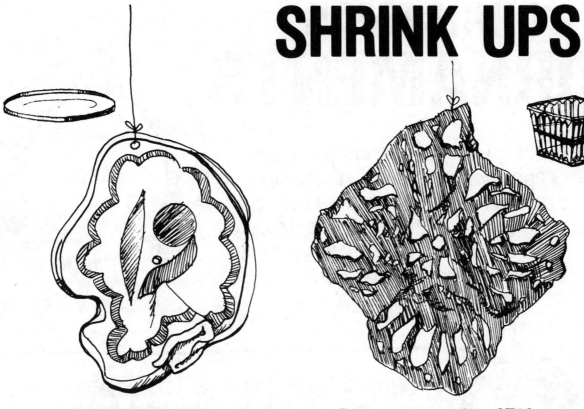

1. Use a **PERMANENT** felt marker to draw designs, pictures, words, etc. on **PLASTIC LIDS** or other pieces of heavy plastic.

2. Poke a hole in the top.

3. Put on a **COOKIE SHEET** in a 200° oven for 15 or 20 minutes. You'll be surprised at what interesting and new shapes you can come up with!

Use your "Shrink Ups" for a mobile, a windchime or as a pendant to hang around your neck.

"Shrink Ups" also make unusual Christmas tree decorations!

1. Take a small **PLASTIC** berry basket and put it on a pie plate.

2. Plastic pill bottles and styrofoam cups are also fun to use.

3. Place in a 200° oven, to bake for just a few minutes. What shape did it melt into? Decorate with glitter, if you wish, and hang on your **CHRISTMAS TREE**, or in a window.

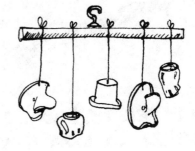

CHRISTMAS ORNAMENTS

Wind strips of green yarn or crepe paper around a wooden curtain ring, plastic ring or cardboard circle. Glue down the end, tie on a perky red ribbon and hang up.

Glue felt or construction paper circles on the inside and back of a jar lid. Decorate the edges with ribbon, felt or crepe paper. Add a Christmas cut-out, or even a picture of each family member.

Decorate a plain or painted pinecone with tiny beads, shiny paper cut-outs, glitter, etc. Hang with yarn or ribbon.

Twist red and white pipecleaners together to look like peppermint candy canes.

GIFT IDEAS

• BUBBLE BATH

• APPLIANCE CORD HOLDER

YOU NEED:

- A jar or small bottle with a lid
- 1 tablespoon of white detergent
- 2 tablespoons of glycerin
- ½ cup of water
- A few drops of cologne
- A few drops of food coloring

YOU DO:

1. Mix all of the ingredients together and then pour the BUBBLE BATH into a bottle.
2. DECORATE the bottle with small cutouts, yarn or "bubble" paint, and tie a perky ribbon around the neck.

YOU NEED:

- An empty cardboard tube
- Scraps of wrapping paper or contact paper
- Paste • Scissors
- Crayons or markers

YOU DO:

1. DECORATE the cardboard tube with crayons, markers or scraps of wrapping paper or contact paper.
2. Then carefully fold up the electric cord and tuck it inside the tube. You will have a HANDY HOLDER for a hair dryer, appliance or extension cord.

CANDLE MAKING

In Colonial days, candles were made by slowly dipping long strings, one at a time, into hot tallow (wax made from animal fat). Today, you can make candles in a jiffy!

YOU NEED:

- Cardboard juice cans, styrofoam cups, milk cartons or greased tin cans
- String
- Pencils or sticks
- Parafin or old candles

YOU DO:

1. For a MOLD, use greased tin cans, juice or milk cartons, or styrofoam cups.

2. To make the WICK, measure string 6 inches longer than your container. Wind it around a pencil or stick and lay across the mold. (Or use a thin candle for a wick, anchoring it in with a little warm wax.)

3. Next, MELT parafin or pieces of used candles in an OLD saucepan or coffee can. Set it in a pan of warm water on the stove at medium heat.*

4. Pour the warm wax CAREFULLY into the container. When the candle is hard (6-8 hours), just peel away the container!

*Be sure that an adult helps.

206

FANCY CANDLES

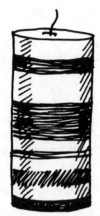

STRIPED CANDLES

For stripes, make layers of different colors. **Let it harden** slightly before pouring the next layer.

SAND CANDLES

Scoop a shape out of sand (at the beach or a sandbox), or pour a little sand into a greased mold. Your finished candle will have a sandy texture.

LACY CANDLES

You can make candles with a delicate pattern by lining the sides of your mold with ice cubes. Then pour warm wax into the middle. The ice will melt, forming a lacy look.

FLOATING CANDLES

Pour an inch of wax into small molds, plastic egg cartons, baking cups or a muffin tin. Stick in a wick when the wax begins to set. Float them in water.

ROOT BEER or CHOCOLATE SODA CANDLES

Pour brown wax into a heavy root beer mug or soda glass (don't forget the wick). Whip some white wax to look like foam or cream and pour on top. Stick in a real drinking straw and mold a red wax cherry for the top!

WHAT OTHER KINDS OF CANDLES CAN YOU CREATE ?

STAINED GLASS COOKIES

You Need:
- ½ cup sugar
- ½ cup honey
- 1½ cups soft margarine
- 1 egg
- 1 teaspoon vanilla

- 2½ cups unsifted flour
- 1 teaspoon baking powder
- ½ teaspoon baking soda
- ½ teaspoon salt
- hard candies, lollipops, etc.

You Do:
1. Blend together sugar, margarine, honey, egg and vanilla in a large bowl.
2. Stir in the baking powder, soda and salt.
3. Cover the dough and chill it for several hours.
4. Cover the baking sheets with foil and draw the outlines of different shapes with a pencil.
5. Roll out snakes or ropes of dough on a floured board. press them around the outlines (or just do them free form).
6. Crush the candy into pieces with a rolling pin. Then spoon different colors into the openings in the dough.
7. Bake at 350 degrees for about 5-6 minutes until the cookies are lightly browned and the candy has melted.
8. Let cool a few minutes, then make holes with a skewer or toothpick for hanging.
9. When completely cool, remove the shapes from the foil and hang them on your tree or in front of a window. Or wrap them in bright paper for a gift.

COOKIE ORNAMENTS
FOR CHRISTMAS GIFTS OR TO HANG ON YOUR TREE

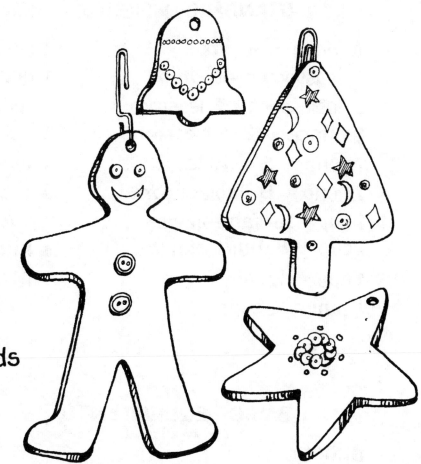

YOU NEED:
- RECIPE

     4 Cups flour
     1 Cup salt
     1½ Cups water

- Waxed paper or foil
- Cookie cutters
- Sequins, buttons, beads
- Shellac and brush
- Paints and brushes

YOU DO:

1. Mix the dough, following the recipe above. Knead thoroughly and add more water if it's too dry. Form your shapes and figures and place them on a cookie sheet; or roll out the dough and cut with holiday cookie cutters.
2. Decorate with sequins. buttons or beads, if you like. Poke a hole through at the top for hanging.
3. Bake at 200° for **ONE HOUR**. Then paint on designs and shellac when completed. **REMEMBER**... these cookies look tempting, but they're **NOT** for eating !
4. After the holidays, carefully wrap each ornament in tissue to save for next year's tree.

MEASURING

STANDARD WEIGHTS & MEASURES

A dash = 8 drops
1 teaspoon = 60 drops
1 Tablespoon = 3 teaspoons
1 ounce = 2 Tablespoons
⅓ cup = 5⅓ Tablespoons
½ cup = 8 Tablespoons
1 cup = 16 Tablespoons
1 cup = 8 fluid ounces
1 cup = ½ pint
1 pint = 2 cups

1 pound = 16 ounces
1 quart = 2 pints
1 gallon = 4 quarts
1 peck = 8 quarts
1 bushel = 4 pecks
1 dram = 1/16 ounce
1 gram = 1/30 ounce
1 kilo = 2.20 pounds
1 liter = approximately 1 quart
1 meter = 39.37 inches

BASIC EQUIVALENTS

Butter:
   1 stick = ½ cup, ¼ pound or 8 Tablespoons

Chocolate:
   1 square = 1 ounce

Uncooked cornmeal or oatmeal:
   1 pound = 3 cups

Eggs:
   1 cup = 5 large ones   1 pound = 9 medium ones

Flour:
   1 pound = 4 cups
   1 cup, sifted = 1 cup plus 2 Tablespoons unsifted

COOKING POEM

COOKING

When you're cooking in the kitchen,
You're learning all the while—
To pour and measure, mix and stir
And sift flour into a pile.

Scrub your hands before you start
Then gather up the **gear**—
Like pots'n pans and measuring cups
That you use throughout the year.

Go over the recipe, step-by-step,
So you'll know just what to do.
By carefully following the **directions,**
It won't be hard for you.

Have a hot pad handy
And an adult standing by—
So you won't hurt yourself
When using the stove or baking a pie.

Besides, the fun and learning,
There's always cleaning up to do,
And even though it's quite a **chore,**
It's part of cooking too.

But after **all** the work is done,
It will soon be time for **dinner.**
And when someone asks for **seconds,**
You'll know you've cooked a winner!

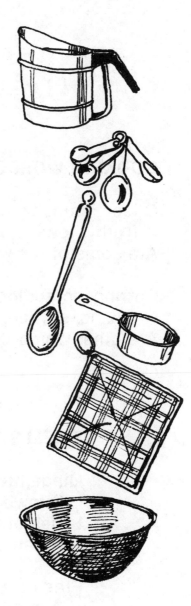

COOKING WORDS

Crispy, crunchy, chewy, munchy
   frothy, foamy, bubbly, punchy
Are some of the words for cooking and eating.

Cutting, shredding, grating, beating,
   mixing, stirring, blending kneading,
Are other words that you'll soon be reading!

SMELLS

Gingerbread and cookies baking in the oven,
   Strawberries, peppermint and Clay.
Lillies of the valley, hyacinths and roses
   A damp woods on a rainy day.

Fresh grass cuttings lying on the ground,
   A musty attic and a rusty old key.
Salty ocean water full of seaweed
   All smell delightful to me.
                                      cbh

COOKING TIPS

1. Here's a great way to pack a *frosted cake* for a picnic. Just bake the cake in a flat pan and cut it in half horizontally. Then spread frosting on top of one layer and top with the second one. Slice into finger-size portions that can be eaten sandwich-style. Take them to the picnic right *in the pan* you baked them in—or wrap each piece individually.

2. Top sliced summer fruit with slightly thawed *lemonade concentrate*—you'll have frosty good flavor in just minutes.

3. Summer vegetables will taste even better if you add a *pinch of sugar* to the water. Brush downward with a damp paper towel to get cornsilk off of an ear of corn.

4. To peel a tomato the easy way, prick the skin with a fork and plunge the tomato into boiling water for 30 seconds. Remove with tongs or a slotted spoon.

5. When marinating food, always use a *glass* or *ceramic dish*—never a stainless steel bowl, aluminum or other metals.

6. When squeezing an orange, lemon or lime, gently roll the fruit on the counter, pressing lightly before slicing it in half and squeezing.

7. To make bread potatoes a *crispy* brown, wash the skins well first, dry and rub them with salad oil before putting in the oven. Brush pie crust with *milk* before baking to make it golden brown.

8. Store sour cream and tomatoes upside-down in the refrigerator.

9. Keep a slice of *fresh bread* in your brown sugar container and store in the refrigerator with a tight lid.

10. If you cover dried fruits and nuts lightly with flour before adding them to your cake batter, they won't sink to the bottom!

HEALTHY FOODS

Too much sugar's not good for you,
　　try honey and nuts and raisins too.
Use **carob** for chocolate, **wheat flour** for white,
　　to provide good nutrition and keep your eyes bright!

Natural foods are the best ones to eat,
　　whole grain cereals with fruit make a morning treat.
Garden vegetables, milk, chicken and fish,
　　and **one** hamburger a week, if you wish.

A trip to a supermarket or health food store
　　to see the **new** products will help you learn more.
About wheat germ, sprouts and Tiger's Milk too—
　　all **tasty** and **healthy** foods for you.

Learn to read **labels** on each box and can
　　to tell you what **un**natural ingredients you should ban.
Look for cracked wheat, graham and stone-ground flour,
　　and unprocessed peanut butter to give you real power!

BANANA SURPRISES

BANANA TID-BITS

You Need:
- 2 bananas
- 3 tablespoons honey
- 1 tablespoon wheat germ
- 3 tablespoons chopped nuts
- toothpicks
- aluminum foil

You Do:
1. cut the bananas into thick slices or chunks.
2. Dip them into the honey and then roll them in the wheat germ and nuts.
3. Place the chunks on a foil-covered cookie sheet and leave in the refrigerator for an hour or so.
4. Keep in plastic bags in the freezer until ready to eat.
5. Poke a toothpike into each one and nibble away. Delicious, and so good for you too!

PEANUT BANANA BARS

You Need:
- ¾ cup soft butter or margarine
- 1 cup dark brown sugar, packed down
- 1 egg
- ½ teaspoon salt
- 1½ cups mashed ripe bananas (about 5 medium sized ones)
- 4 cups uncooked regular oats
- 1 cup raisins
- ½ cup chopped cocktail peanuts

You Do:
1. In a large bowl beat the butter and sugar until light and fluffy.
2. Beat in the egg, salt and banana and stir in the remaining ingredients.
3. Turn into a greased 13x9x2 inch baking pan. Bake in 350° oven 1 hour, or until cake tester inserted in center comes out clean. Let cool; then cut into 2x1 inch bars. Yield: 58 bars.

HEALTHY SNACKS

PROTEIN GEMS

You Need:
- ½ cup of crunchy natural peanut butter
- ½ cup of honey
- ½ cup of raw oatmeal
- ½ cup of sesame seeds
- ½ cup of walnuts or almonds
- ¼ cup of wheat germ
- ½ cup of protein (vanilla or chocolate) available at health food stores
- ¼ cup of unsweetened coconut

You Do:
1. Mix all of the ingredients together and shape into balls.
2. Roll in some grated coconut and refrigerate.
   A Delicious, Healthy Snack!

CEREAL NIBBLES

You Need:
- 2½ cups golden graham cereal
- ½ cup dry roasted peanuts
- 2 tablespoons butter or margarine
- ½ cup raisins
- 2 tablespoons peanut butter
- pinch of cinnamon

You Do:
1. Mix the cereal and peanuts together in a bowl.
2. Melt the butter, peanut butter, raisins and cinnamon, and add to the cereal mixture.
3. Bake at 350 degrees for 10 minutes.
4. When cool, cut into squares or break into small pieces.

CHEESE CRUNCHIES

CHEESE CRUNCHIES

You Need:
- ½ cup butter or margarine (1 stick)
- 1 cup all purpose flour (sifted)
- 1 cup shredded cheddar cheese
- Pinch of salt
- 1 cup rice cereal bits

You Do:
1. Cut up the butter into 6 or 8 slices and mix together with the flour, cheese and salt. Use your fingers or a fork.
2. Knead in the cereal bits; then roll the dough into small *balls* or *snakes.* Press them down flat and place on an ungreased cookie sheet.
3. Bake for about 10 minutes in a 375° oven.

EASY CHEESE CRISPIES

You Need:
- 1 cup of grated cheddar cheese
- ½ stick of softened butter
- ½ cup sifted flour
- pinch of salt

You Do:
1. Mix all ingredients together with a pastry blender or your hands.
2. Knead and form into small balls.
3. Place on a cookie sheet about an inch apart, and bake for 12 minutes, in a 375° oven.

EASY GORP COOKIES
(Makes 3 dozen cookies)

You Need:

- 1 cup of butter or margarine
- 1 cup of brown sugar
- 1 cup of white flour
- 1 cup of whole wheat flour
- 1 teaspoon baking soda
- 2 teaspoons milk
- ½ cup raisins
- ½ cup peanuts
- ½ cup peanuts
- ¼ cup carob or chocolate chips

You Do:
1. Cream together the margarine and sugar.
2. Then add the flour, soda and milk, mixing well.
3. Mix in the raisins, peanuts and chips.
4. Drop the dough by tablespoonfuls onto a greased cookie sheet and bake at 350º for 8 to 10 minutes.
5. Let cool, then lift off of the cookie sheet with a spatula.

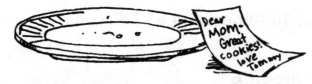

OATS AND COCONUT GRANOLA BARS

You Need:
- 2 cups of Quick Oats, uncooked
- ⅓ cup melted butter or margarine
- ¼ cup honey
- ⅔ cup shredded or flaked coconut
- ⅓ cup brown sugar
- pinch of salt

You Do:
1. Toast the oats in a jelly roll pan 9x13 in a preheated 350 degree oven for 18 to 20 minutes.
2. Cool and combine with the remaining ingredients.
3. Mix well, then press firmly into the jelly roll pan.
4. Bake at 400 degrees for 15 to 18 minutes until golden brown and bubbly.
5. When cool, cut into bars and store in a loosely covered container.

218

SUPER COOKIES

Super cookies are great for camping trips or anytime you feel like having a little something for a quick surge of energy. When you reach into your cookie jar, here's a treat that will not only bring smiles and satisfy your "sweet tooth" but will provide nourishment as well.

You Need:
- 1 egg
- ½ cup honey
- ¼ cup safflower oil
- ½ cup whole wheat pastry flour (available at Health Food Stores)
- 1 Tablespoon powdered milk
- 1 cup rolled oats
- 2 Tablespoons wheat germ
- 3 Tablespoons sunflower seeds
- 2 Tablespoons sesame seeds
- 2 Tablespoons cashew pieces
- ½ cup raisins
- ¼ teaspoon sea salt
- 1 teaspoon vanilla
- a pinch of cinnamon

You Do:
1. Place the egg in a mixing bowl and beat lightly. Stir in honey and oil.
2. Add all remaining ingredients and mix well.
3. Place batter by tablespoonfuls on a buttered cookie sheet.
4. Flatten the cookies slightly with your fingers or the back of a spoon.
5. Bake in a preheated 300° oven for 30 minutes, or until golden.
6. Cool on wire racks. Store in airtight container.

YUMMY CANDY TREAT

You Need:
- 1 cup honey
- 1 cup peanut butter
- 2 cups powdered milk
- 1 cup raisins
- ½ cup sunflower seeds
- ½ cup toasted wheat germ

You Do:
1. Mix together all of the ingredients except the wheat germ and form into small balls.
2. Roll in the toasted wheat germ and refrigerate.

GRAHAM CRACKERS

Did you know that graham crackers are one of the earliest health foods? They became popluar in the 19th century when a preacher named Sylvester Graham went around the United States telling people how nutritious whole wheat was.

What's your favorite graham cracker treat? Most kids would probably say, **S'MORES!**

1. All you need is a toasted marshmallow, and some squares of chocolate, sandwiched between two graham crackers.
2. This gooey dessert treat is *so* good (although Rev. Graham wouldn't approve of the sugar) that everyone always begs for "some more!"

HOMEMADE GRAHAM CRACKERS

You Need:
- ½ cup butter
- ⅔ cup brown sugar
- 2¾ cup graham flour
- ½ teaspoon salt
- ½ teaspoon baking powder
- ¼ teaspoon cinnamon
- ½ cup water

You Do:
1. Cream the butter and sugar together.
2. Mix the remaining ingredients (except the water) and add them to the creamed mixture. Slowly stir in the water, a little at a time.
3. After mixing well, let the dough stand for about 30 minutes.
4. Then roll it out on a floured board to 1/8 inch thickness and cut into 2-inch squares.
5. Place on a greased cookie sheet and bake for 20 minutes in a 350⁰ oven.

S'MORES INDOORS

You Need:
- 1 package (11½ ounces) of chocolate or carob bits
- ⅔ cup light corn syrup
- 2 tablespoons margarine or butter
- 1 teaspoon vanilla
- 1 package (10 ounces) of graham cracker cereal
- 3 cups miniature marshmallows

You Do:
1. Place the chocolate bits, corn syrup and margarine in a 3 quart saucepan and bring to a boil, stirring constantly.
2. Remove from the heat and stir in the vanilla.
3. Pour the cereal in a large bowl; then mix in the chocolate, tossing until well coated.
4. Add the marshmallows, one cup at a time.
5. Press the mixture into a greased pan (13x9x2) and let stand for about an hour until firm.
6. Cut into squares and enjoy.

FESTIVE GRAHAM CRACKER ICEBOX CAKE

You Need:
- 1 cup of heavy cream
- 2 Tablespoons sugar or honey
- 32 graham cracker squares

You Do:
1. Beat the cream and honey together until stiff.
2. Spread the cream on top of a graham cracker, then top with another one and spread cream on that. Do this until you have four crackers stacked up.
3. Make 8 stacks in all. Then gently press down on each one until cream squeezes out of the sides. Use your knife to "frost" the cream around the sides of each stack.
4. Push the stacks together to make a square/cake.
5. Frost the top with any leftover whipped cream; refrigerate for several hours, then top with sprinkles, carob chips or colored sugar and serve.

You can make a chocolate cake roll the same way using chocolate wafers.

APPLE IDEAS

MAKE YOUR OWN APPLESAUCE

You Need:
- 4 apples
- ⅓ cup sugar
- 1 tablespoon cinnamon
- strainer
- ½ cup water
- spoon and knife
- saucepan
- hot pad

You Do:
1. Wash, core and cut up the apples and place them in a saucepan with ½ cup water.
2. Cook over low heat for 10-15 minutes, stirring occasionally until the apples become mushy.
3. Remove from the stove and drain through a strainer. Return the mixture to the pan, add sugar and cinnamon, and simmer for 3 more minutes, stirring gently.
4. You can eat your applesauce while it is still warm, or refrigerate it for later. The whole family will enjoy eating what you have made — for lunch, dinner or a snack.

ONION-APPLE SAUCE

Did you ever think that apples and onions would taste good together? Here's a recipe that will show you that they do.

You Need:
- three apples
- three onions
- three teaspoons of oil

cinnamon, cloves
sugar

You Do:
1. Peel, core and slice up the apples; then peel and slice the onions.
2. Pour the oil into a saucepan, and add the apples and onions.
3. Fry for a few minutes on medium heat, turning a few times, until soft and golden.
4. Sprinkle the mixture with cinnamon, cloves and sugar, to taste.
5. Cool and try out this new taste treat. Serve it to your family or friends and see what they think.

APPLE BUTTER

You Need:
- 4 lbs. apples
- ¼ cup water
- ¼ cup apple cider vinegar
- ½ cup brown sugar
- 1 teaspoon cinnamon
- ½ teaspoon cloves (ground)

You Do:
1. Core and quarter unpeeled apples, then chop up or put in blender with water and vinegar.
2. Cook in a saucepan over low heat until the mixture gets thick and turns brown. Stir occasionally. This will take 2-3 hours (¼ of that time in a microwave oven)
3. Add sugar and spices and cook for ½ hour more.
4. Refrigerate, then spread on toast or muffins.

APPLE COOKIES

You Need:
- ¼ cup unsalted butter
- ¼ cup safflower oil
- ¾ cup honey
- 2 eggs
- 1¼ cup whole wheat pastry flour
- 2 tablespoons baking soda
- ½ teaspoon cinnamon
- ¾ cup wheat germ
- ½ cup uncooked oatmeal
- 1 cup finely chopped peeled and cored apples

You Do:
1. Cream the butter in the oil; then add the honey and eggs.
2. Mix the dry ingredients and combine with the creamed mixture.
3. Stir in the apples and drop spoonfuls of the dough onto a greased cookie sheet.
4. Bake for 10-15 minutes at 350 degrees.

APPLE SNACKS

Stuffed Apple

Core, then stuff opening with peanut butter mixed with raisins, wheat germ or granola. Slice in half and wrap in plastic, or store in a sandwich bag.

CAROB TREATS

Carob can be found in health food stores and in some groceries. It is low in sugar and has no caffeine. You might try mixing ½ carob and ½ cocoa to begin with.

CAROB CANDY

You Need:
- 1 cup carob chips or nuggets
- ¼ cup honey
- ½ cup canned, evaporated milk
- ½ cup chopped walnuts
- Saucepan, wooden spoon

You Do:
1. Put carob, honey & milk in a pan and cook over low heat for 20 minutes, stirring with a wooden spoon.
2. Cool, then place in refrigerator for an hour.
3. Shape into balls and roll in the chopped walnuts.

SUPER FUDGE

You Need:
- ½ cup honey
- ½ cup cocoa or carob powder
- ½ cup raisins or dates
- ½-1 cup shredded coconut
- ½ cup peanut butter
- 2 cups chopped nuts, sunflower or sesame seeds

You Do:
1. Place the honey and peanut butter in a pan and heat until blended.
2. Quickly stir in the carob or cocoa powder.
3. Remove from the stove and add the remaining ingredients.
4. Pour into a square, greased pan and refrigerate.
5. Cut into squares and eat!

CAROB CHIP COOKIES

You Need:
- 2¼ cups whole wheat pastry flour
- 1 teaspoon salt
- 1 teaspoon baking soda
- 1 cup butter
- ½ cup molasses (unsulphered)
- ¾ cup honey
- 1 teaspoon vanilla
- 1 cup oatmeal
- 1 teaspoon water
- 1 cup pecans
- 2 cups carob chips
- 2 eggs

You Do:
1. Mix the flour, salt and soda in a bowl.
2. Then mix the rest of the ingredients and add them to the flour mixture.
3. Drop by spoonfuls onto a greased cookie sheet and bake at 375 degrees until **crisp** (approximately 13 minutes).

SHRINKING SNAKES

You Need:
- ½ cup of peanut butter
- ½ cup of honey
- ½ teaspoon vanilla extract
- ¼ cup raisins
- 2 heaping tablespoons shredded coconut
- ½ cup of dry milk powder
- a heaping tablespoon of carob powder or cocoa
- ¼ cup of chopped nuts and chopped dates

You Do:
1. Blend together the milk and peanut butter.
2. Stir in the other ingredients, one at a time. (Your hands or a wooden spoon will do the job best!)
3. Place the mixture on a piece of waxed paper and roll into one **long snake,** or lots of short ones.
4. Cut the roll into small pieces and wrap each one in waxed paper of some plastic wrap. Store in the refrigerator. (Or leave your snake **as is** and tear off bits to eat from time to time.)

DOC PIZZO SAYS

1. *Natural* foods are better for us than processed ones, so eat an *apple* instead of apple pie!
2. The *best* foods to eat are:
   • whole grain cereals
   • fresh fruits and vegetables
   • eggs, milk and fish for protein
   • chicken, turkey and fish instead of beef, pork and lamb
   • safflower, peanut, sesame and olive oil are better for you than fat, lard and butter
   • candy bars with honey, carob, nuts and raisins
   • home-made margarine (see recipe) is better than butter with added dye.
   • fresh fruit juices
   • water is the best drink of all!

Hints
1. Avoid processed foods, preservatives and additives.
2. When substituting *honey* for *sugar* in a recipe, use an equal amount, but less liquid (¼ cup per cup of honey). Lower oven temperature about 25 degrees.
3. Before measuring honey, wet the spoon or cup with oil or melted butter. Never keep honey in the refrigerator - it will get grainy.
4. The best *grains* are: cracked wheat, wheat grits, whole wheat and graham flour; oat groats, steel cut rolled oats, scotch oatmeal, whole wheat oat flour; bran flakes, wheat germ (must be fresh) and wheat germ flour.
5. Store all natural grains, flour and seeds in the refrigerator or freezer!

TO MAKE YOUR OWN SOFT MARGARINE,
1. Mix equal parts of pure butter with equal parts of cold pressed or safflower oil.
2. OR, mix one part butter with three parts safflower or other oil.

DOC'S SPECIAL GRIDDLE CAKES (with "make ahead of time batter")

You Need:

- 1½ cups whole wheat flour
- 1¾ teaspoon baking powder
- ½ teaspoon salt
- 3 tablespoons honey

- 2 eggs
- 3 tablespoons safflower or corn oil
- 1 cup milk

You Do:
1. Combine the dry ingredients in a large bowl.
2. Beat the eggs and add the honey, oil and milk. Pour into the large bowl and mix until barely moistened.
3. Cover and let set in a cool place (overnight, if possible).
4. Bake on a lightly greased griddle or frying pan.
5. When you see bubbles, turn the pancakes and brown the second side.

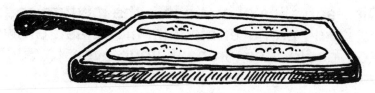

DOC PIZZO'S ADD-ONS

Make your **pancakes, muffins** and **waffles** even more delicious by adding chopped raisins and nuts, grated orange rind or fresh berries* to the batter.

For a more nutritious batter, replace part of the flour with wheat germ, brewer's yeast, soy flour or corn meal.

*For best results, let the batter "sit" for about ½ hour before stirring in berries.

Try these toppings: fresh fruits, maple syrup, honey mixed with cinnamon, peanut butter or yogurt, or apple sauce with yogurt or sour cream.

FRENCH TOAST

You Need:
- 1 egg
- ⅓ cup milk
- 3 slices of whole wheat bread
- 1 teaspoon honey
- 1/4 teaspoon vanilla

You Do:
1. Beat the egg lightly and then add the milk, honey and vanilla.
2. Dip each slice of bread into the mixture and transfer to a well greased frying pan over medium-high heat. Brown on both sides.
3. You could also preheat your oven to 500° and bake the soaked bread on a greased pan, turning once.

MAKE YOUR OWN FRENCH FRIES

1. Scrub and cut unpeeled Idaho potatoes in sections lengthwise.
2. Drop them into a bowl of icewater for 10-20 minutes. (This will make them brown better and absorb less fat).
3. Drain and place in a bowl with ¼ T of oil for each one (coat them well).
4. Sprinkle with paprika - stir and place on a lightly oiled cookie pan.
5. Bake at 450° for 20-25 minutes until golden brown.

Thanks to Dr. Albert J. Pizzo
Doc Pizzo's Nutrition Handbook
California: Children's Foundation, 1977

MICROWAVE MUNCHIES

NACHOS

You Need:
- 4 cups large corn chips
- 1 cup shredded cheddar cheese
- ½ teaspoon hot sauce

You Do:
1. Spread the chips on a platter.
2. Sprinkle cheese evenly over the top and hot sauce over the cheese.
3. Cook on high for 2 to 3 minutes or until cheese is melted.

PIZZA CRACKERS

You Need:
- 6 saltine crackers
- 2 Tablespoons pizza sauce
- ⅛ teaspoon onion salt
- ¼ cup shredded mozzarella cheese
- ¼ teaspoon Italian seasoning

You Do:
1. Cover a plate with a paper towel.
2. Arrange 6 crackers in a circle on the towel.
3. Combine the pizza sauce and onion salt and place a well-rounded teaspoon of sauce on each cracker.
4. Sprinkle shredded cheese over each and a little Italian seasoning over the top.
5. Cook on high for 30 to 45 seconds or until the cheese melts.

FAVORITE FOODS

HOT DOGS

Everyone loves frankfurters, better known as "franks" or "hotdogs." Here are some different ways to enjoy them:

1. Cut the franks up into chunks and broil on skewers, along with tiny tomatoes, onions, pitted ripe olives, pineapple chunks and bacon.
2. Stick toothpicks through tiny hotdogs and dip into ketchup or mustard sauce.
3. Combine with soup, beans or spaghetti.
4. Layer slices in a casserole with potatoes, cheese, milk, butter and flour.
5. Sprinkle small pieces into your pancake or waffle batter.
6. Great in omelettes or scrambled eggs!

And, of course, as part of a *sandwich* they can't be beat!

1. Slit a hotdog lengthwise, stuff with cheese and wrap in bacon secured by a toothpick. Broil or barbecue.
2. Roll them up inside corn or flour tortillas and serve with guacamole dip.
3. For a sandwich spread, grind up the meat and mix with chopped celery and onion, mayonnaise and mustard.
4. Top half of an English muffin with pizza sauce, frank slices and cheese, and pop under the broiler. Yum!

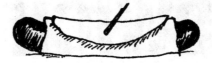

MEXICAN HOT DOGS

You Need:
- 1 pound of hot dogs
- ½ lb. cheese (longhorn or cheddar)
- 1 package corn tortillas
- 1 small can of green chilies

You Do:
1. Slice the chiles and cheese into long strips.
2. Cut the hotdogs on one side, lengthwise and place a cheese slice inside.
3. Put the hotdog and a chile slice on a corn tortilla and roll.
4. Insert a toothpick to keep together.
5. Deep fry or bake until the tortilla and wiener are cooked.

SAUSAGE BISCUITS

You Need:
- A tube of refrigerator biscuits
- Hotdogs or sausages
- ½ lb. cheddar cheese, grated

You Do:
1. Cut the hotdogs or sausages into bite-size pieces.
2. Pull apart the biscuit dough and place on a cookie sheet.
3. Place a sausage bit in the **middle** of each biscuit and sprinkle some cheese over the top.
4. Roll the dough around the sausage and bake for 10-12 minutes in a 450 degree oven.
   Sausage biscuits are also delicious when cooked on a green stick over a charcoal grill or open fire.

SANDWICH FUN

APPLE SANDWICHES

1. Cut an apple into small chunks.
2. Add bacon bits and cottage cheese and mix well.
3. Spread the apple mixture on slices of whole wheat bread.

SUPER SANDWICHES

1. Use whole wheat or rye bread, or wheat flour rolls sliced in half.
2. Spread with margarine or mayonnaise; add some lettuce, and heap on slices of turkey, ham, bologna, cheese, hardboiled eggs, tomato, a pickle and so forth.
3. Sprinkle some alfalfa sprouts, chopped nuts and wheat germ on top. Open your mouth wide, and enjoy!

PEANUT BUTTER AND JELLY COOKIE-WICHES

You Need:
- ½ cup butter or margarine
- ½ cup chunky peanut butter
- ½ cup sugar
- ½ cup brown sugar
- 1 egg
- 1½ **cups of** all-purpose flour
- ¾ teaspoon baking soda
- ½ teaspoon baking powder
- ¼ teaspoon salt
- jelly or jam

You Do:
1. Mix together butter, peanut butter and both sugars. Then blend in everything else except the jelly.
2. Cover and chill the dough before shaping into small balls.
3. Bake at 350° for 12-15 minutes.
4. When cool, spread jelly on one cookie and top with another for your cookie-wiches.

PIZZAS

MUFFIN PIZZAS

You Need:
- English Muffins
- Tomato Sauce
- Slices of mushroom, sausage, olives, green pepper
- Spices
- Mozzarella or American cheese

You Do:
1. Cut an English muffin in half, place on a baking sheet and spread a tomato mixture on top. (Make your own from tomato sauce and some spices like chopped onion, oregano and basil or use chili sauce).
2. Press in pieces of mushroom, slices of sausage, olives, and green pepper (or whatever else you like best).
3. Pop into a 450° oven for about 10 minutes.
4. Sprinkle mozzarella or American cheese on top and put back in oven until it melts.

APPLE PIZZAS

You Need:
- 2 tablespoons flour
- ½ cup of firmly packed brown sugar
- ½ teaspoon cinnamon
- a can of refrigerator biscuits
- 1 cup of grated mild cheese
- 2 apples, peeled   • a dab of margarine or butter

You Do:
1. Measure the flour, sugar and cinnamon into a small bowl. Mix well.
2. Press or roll the biscuits into flat circles and place on a lightly greased cookie sheet.
3. Sprinkle with grated cheese.
4. Slice up the apples and arrange on top of the cheese.
5. Spoon on the brown sugar mixture, dot with butter or margarine and bake at 350 degrees for 20-30 minutes.
6. Let cool before eating. Delicious!

233

ALL ABOUT POPCORN

Legend tells us that an Indian named Quadequina, the chief's brother, brought a small pouch of parched corn seeds to the first Thanksgiving feast.

When he threw a few of the seeds or kernels into the fire, some of them began popping! That was the beginning of a delicous treat, popcorn, loved by old and young alike.

POPCORN FACTS

1. Popcorn is one of our most **nutritious foods:**
One 30 gram serving is 7.6% protein, 28.7% fat and 56% carbohydrate ...as well as containing calcium, phosphorus, iron, B complex and vitamin E, riboflavin and thiamine!
2. Popcorn dates back 80,000 years to **Mexico** where fossils of corn pollen have been found in diggings below Mexico City. It is thought that the ancient dwellers popped it on a stick over a **fire** (much as we do marshmallows), or in pottery or metal containers. Sometimes they placed the kernels right on the **hot coals**, letting them pop out onto the ground. You might want to try that at your next campfire.
3. Indian tribes in North and South America planted, ate and used popcorn for decorations and jewelry long **before** explorers landed in the New World.
4. The American colonists enjoyed popcorn for breakfast with sugar and cream!
5. If you use an electric hot-air popper or a microwave oven, you can pop your corn **without** oil. There are only 23 calories in a plain cup of popcorn.
6. Today a company in Australia makes a popcorn product called, **"Lolly Gobble Bliss Bombs,"** packaged in a purple box!

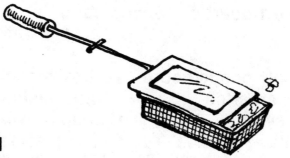

POPPING CORN

Pop up a batch of corn in a heavy saucepan with a lid, or an electric skillet or popper (use 3 Tablespoonfuls of oil and ⅓ cup of popcorn in a 3 quart popper; ¼ cup of oil and ½ cup of popcorn in a 4 quart one).

You Do:
1. A good method is to pour the oil into a warm popper; then place one kernel of corn in the middle. Cook over medium-high heat. When the kernel pops, pour in the rest of the popcorn, and stir or shake it until mixed.
2. Then put on the cover, leaving a tiny air space, and shake the pan gently over the heat.
3. Listen to the pops! When you hear only a few, your popcorn is done.
4. Pour into a bowl, drizzle melted butter or margarine and some salt over it, and toss well.
5. For a different taste, sprinkle some grated American cheese and bacon bits over the buttered corn.

Note: One pound of kernels will make 8-10 quarts of popped corn.

PEANUT BUTTER POPCORN BALLS

You Need:
- 8 cups popcorn
- ½ stick margarine
- 1 large package marshmallows
- ¾ cup peanut butter
- ½ cup wheat germ
- ½ cup chocolate or carob chips

You Do:
1. Place everything, except the popcorn, in a pot and stir over a low heat until melted.
2. Then pour over the popcorn. Butter your hands before making the balls.

235

GRANOLA POPCORN BALLS
(2 tablespoons make 1 quart of popped corn)

You Need:
- 2½ quarts of freshly popped corn
- ¼ cup butter or margarine
- ½ cup light corn syrup
- ½ teaspoon vanilla
- 1 box granola cereal (with raisins & dates)
- 1 cup brown sugar
- ⅔ cup sweetened condensed milk
- ¼ cup toasted sesame seeds

You Do:
1. Melt the butter, then stir in the brown sugar, syrup and milk. Heat until it boils, stirring constantly.
2. Reduce heat and keep on stirring until mixture comes to the soft ball stage.
3. Stir in the vanilla.
4. Mix together the popcorn, granola and sesame seeds in a large bowl and pour the syrupy mixture over it.
5. Butter your hands a little and shape the popcorn into balls. Yum! CRUNCH, MUNCH!

GELATIN POPCORN BALLS

You Need:
- 1 cup light corn syrup
- ½ cup sugar
- 1 package fruit flavored gelatin
- ½ pound peanuts
- 9 cups popped corn

You Do:
1. Bring the sugar and syrup to a boil.
2. Remove from the stove and add the gelatin, stirring well.
3. Add the peanuts and pour the mixture over the popcorn.
4. Form into balls.

CARAMEL CORN

You Need:
- ½ package (14 oz.) of caramels
- 1/8 cup of light corn syrup
- 1 Tablespoon water
- a quart of popcorn

You Do:
- Melt the caramels, corn syrup and water in the top of a double boiler, stirring occasionally.
- Pour over the popcorn and form into balls.

HONEY POPCORN

You Need:
- ½ cup of honey
- ¼ cup margarine or butter
- 6 cups of popped corn
- 1 cup of shelled peanuts

You Do:
1. Heat the honey and margarine until well blended.
2. Cool and pour over the popcorn and peanuts. Stir well.
3. Spread out in a pan and bake for 5 to 10 minutes in a 350⁰ oven. Stir several times, until crispy.
4. Spoon into a large bowl or individual plastic bags.

POPCORN POEM

Popcorn's a snack food that's **good** for you.
It has **fiber** and **protein** and **vitamins** too.
If you leave off the butter, the **calories** are low,
And it's such **fun** to pop, as you undoubtedly know!

PEANUT BUTTER

PEANUT BUTTER SNACKS

You Need:
- 1 cup peanut butter-flavored baking chips
- ¼ cup chunky peanut butter
- 2 Tablespoons butter
- 3 cups chow mein noodles

You Do:
1. Combine the peanut butter chips, peanut butter and butter in a 1-quart glass measuring cup.
2. Cook on high for 2½ to 3 minutes.
3. Stir until smooth;then stir in the chow mein noodles.
4. Drop by spoonfuls onto waxed paper.
5. Chill until firm and serve.

PEANUT BUTTER KISSES

You Need:
- 1⅓ cups of flour
- ½ teaspoon of salt
- ⅓ cup peanut butter
- 1 egg
- 1 teaspoon vanilla
- 1 teaspoon of baking soda
- ½ cup butter or margarine
- ¾ cup brown sugar (1/8 cup for later)
- chocolate kisses

You Do:
1. Sift the flour, baking soda and salt into a bowl.
2. In another bowl, cream the butter and peanut butter; then add the sugar and beat well.
3. Mix in the vanilla, eggs and the sifted ingredients.
4. Chill the dough for an hour; then shape into balls and roll in brown sugar.
5. Bake on an ungreased cookie sheet at 375 degrees for 8 minutes.
6. Carefully remove the cookies from the oven, press a chocolate kiss into each one and bake for 2 minutes more.
(This recipe makes about 30 cookies.)

TOASTED PEANUT-BREAD "CANDY" BARS

You Need:
- 1 loaf whole wheat bread, sliced
- 1 pkg. peanuts (raw are best), chopped
- 1 cup natural peanut butter, thinned with peanut oil
- ½ cup toasted wheat germ, carob (optional)

You Do:
1. Trim off the bread crusts, then cut slices in half.
2. Place both bread & crusts on a cookie sheet in the 150° oven for ½ hour (or leave in closed unlit oven overnight).
3. Crumble the crusts in a blender.
4. Combine with chopped nuts and wheat germ.
5. Dip the bread slices in the peanut butter and then in the crumbs mixture.
6. Dry on a cookie sheet and store in an airtight container.

Optional Yummy — After coating the toast with peanut butter, dip in melted carob and then in the nuts and crumb mixture.

And while you are learning about metrics, here's a fun recipe to try that uses grams and milliliters:

METRIC PEANUT BUTTER BALLS

You Need:
- 2 egg yolks
- 5 milliliters of vanilla
- 1 gram salt
- 235 grams crunchy peanut butter
- 140 grams powdered milk
- 250 grams powdered sugar

You Do:
1. Beat the egg yolks, vanilla and salt together in a bowl.
2. Add the peanut butter, milk and sugar and mix well.
3. Knead with your fingers until firm, then shape into balls and roll in some powdered sugar.

Can you turn this recipe back into teaspoons, tablespoons and cups?

FUN DESSERTS

BROWNIE CUPCAKES

You Need:
- 1½ cups cake flour
- 1 teaspoon baking soda
- ½ cup butter or margarine
- 1 cup brown sugar
- 1 egg
- 1 oz. or square unsweetened chocolate
- ½ cup buttermilk
- ¼ teaspoon vanilla

You Do:
1. Preheat oven to 350°.
2. Sift together the flour and baking soda.
3. Cream the butter and brown sugar; then beat in the egg.
4. Melt the chocolate and add it to the batter.
5. Slowly beat in the flour and buttermilk, then stir in the vanilla.
6. Place paper baking cups in a muffin tin and spoon in the batter (½ full). Or pour 1 heaping teaspoonful into miniature cupcake tins.
7. Bake 10-15 minutes.
8. Remove from tins and cool on a rack, before frosting.

— from "Reese Cooks"

PUDDING COOKIES

You Need:
- 1 4 oz. package of instant pudding
- 1 cup of biscuit mix
- ¼ cup of vegetable shortening
- 1 egg
- 3 Tablespoons milk

You Do:
1. Combine the pudding with the biscuit mix and cut in the shortening.
2. Then stir in the eggs and milk and blend well.
3. Drop on an ungreased cookie sheet by teaspoonfuls and bake at 350⁰ for 8-10 minutes until brown.

PARTY FOODS

OLD FASHIONED TAFFY

You Need:
- 4 cups sugar
- 1 teaspoon cream of tartar
- 1½ cups water
- flavoring and coloring to taste

You Do:
1. Mix the sugar and cream of tartar together.
2. Heat the water in a saucepan until it boils; then pour in the sugar and cream of tartar, stirring until it dissolves.
3. Let boil until threads form from a hot spoon.
4. When firm, pour out into a chilled, buttered slab or platter.
5. Using a spatula, turn the edges to the center until it is cool.
6. Break into pieces and start pulling!

CARAMEL APPLES

You Need:
- 6 apples
- 1 package (14 oz.) of light-colored caramels
- 6 wooden skewers or popsicle sticks
- ¼ cup evaporated milk

Optional:
- walnuts (finely chopped) flaked coconut

You Do:
1. Heat the caramels and evaporated milk in the top of a double boiler, stirring occasionally, until the caramel sauce is smooth. Remove from heat.
2. Push a stick through the **bottom** of each apple.
3. *Then **carefully** dip the apples, one at a time, into the caramel sauce, turning the apple so it coats evenly. Hold it over the pot until the excess caramel drips back.
4. For an **extra treat,** spread the walnuts and/or coconut flakes onto a sheet of waxed paper and roll your caramel apple in them.
5. When cool, wrap each apple in plastic or eat and enjoy!

*Be sure an adult is nearby.

BAKE-A-CAKE

PEANUT BUTTER and JELLY CAKE

You Need:
- 1 stick of margarine
- 1⅓ cups of sugar
- ¼ cup crunchy or smooth peanut butter
- 1 teaspoon vanilla
- 2 eggs
- 2 cups flour
- 1 Tablespoon baking powder
- 1 teaspoon salt
- 1 cup milk
- ⅓ cup grape jelly

(Note: For a lighter texture, use smooth peanut butter.)

You Do:
1. Cream the margarine. Gradually add the sugar, beating thoroughly.
2. Add peanut butter, vanilla and eggs and beat well.
3. Sift together flour, baking powder and salt. Add to creamed mixture alternately with milk, mixing well after each addition.
4. Pour into two greased and floured 8-or 9-inch layer pans. Bake in 350-degree oven for 35 to 40 minutes.
5. Cool, then spread jelly between the layers. Frost sides and top with peanut butter frosting.

CRAZY CAKE

You Need:
- 1 cup sugar
- 1½ cups flour
- ½ teaspoon salt
- 3 tablespoons cocoa
- 1 teaspoon soda
- 5 tablespoons salad oil
- 1 tablespoon vinegar
- 1 teaspoon vanilla
- 1 cup cold water

You Do:
1. Sift the dry ingredients and then pour in the oil, vinegar and vanilla, mixing well.
2. Pour into an 8x8 pan and bake at 350° for 35-40 minutes.

PEANUT BUTTER FROSTING

You Need:
- ¼ cup (½ stick) margarine
- ¼ cup peanut butter
- 1 teaspoon vanilla
- ½ teaspoon salt
- 2½ cups sifted confectioners' sugar
- 3 Tablespoons milk

You Do:
1. Cream the margarine and blend in the peanut butter, vanilla and salt.
2. Add sugar alternately with milk, beating until light and fluffy.

LEMON CREAM CHEESE FROSTING

You Need:
- 1 package cream cheese (8 oz.)
- ½ cup soft butter
- 1 cup honey
- 1 tablespoon lemon juice
- 1 tablespoon lemon peel
- 1 teaspoon vanilla
- a dash of salt

You Do:
1. Leave the cream cheese at room temperature until soft; then mix it with the butter.
2. Add the honey, lemon juice and peel, vanilla and salt.
3. Beat until fluffy and use to frost an apple-nut or carrot cake.

For an unusual snack, spread the frosting on apple slices and sprinkle some nuts on top.

HOMEMADE ICE CREAM

ICE CREAM SCOOPS

1. **Homemade** ice cream is rich, creamy and oh, so good!
2. Ice cream was invented about 300 years ago by either the French or the Italians (no one is quite sure).
3. **Vanilla** is the most popular flavor, probably because it goes so well with many kinds of toppings.
4. You can use a crank-type **machine** or an electric **mixer** and your own **freezer** to make delicious home-made ice cream.
5. Home-made ice cream can be **stored** up to a month in your freezer. After that it tends to lose its good texture and taste.
6. Light cream or half-and-half can be substituted for heavy cream or whipping cream, but the ice cream won't be as **fluffy** or **smooth.**

So enjoy whipping up a few batches of home-made ice cream. It's fun, less expensive and better for you too.

EASY STRAWBERRY ICE CREAM

You Need:
- 1 pint of fresh strawberries
- 1 cup of sugar
- 1 tablespoon lemon juice
- ½ cup cream
- ½ cup of milk

You Do:
1. Wash and hull the strawberries; then crush up in a large bowl (a potato masher works well.)
2. Add the sugar and let stand for about 10 minutes.
3. Stir in the lemon juice, cream and milk.
4. Pour into a freezer tray. When partially frozen, remove and spoon into a large bowl.
5. Whip with an electric beater (or by hand) until stiff.
6. Refreeze for an hour or so, then eat. Delicious!

EASY LEMON SHERBET

You Need:
- juice of 2 large lemons
- grated rind of 1 lemon
- 2 cups of sugar
- 4 cups of milk

You Do:
1. Add the juice and rind to the sugar, then slowly mix with the milk.
2. Pour into refrigerator trays and partially freeze.
3. Stir to break up the large crystals before freezing completely.

WATERMELON SHERBET

You Need:
- 6 cups of ripe watermelon
- 1 cup of sugar
- ½ lemon

You Do:
1. Cut up chunks of watermelon, remove the seeds and blend with the sugar in blender or food processor.
2. Squeeze the lemon and add the juice and stir well.
3. Spoon into an ice cube tray and place in freezer, for about 1½ hours.
4. Remove and beat until smooth, then return to freezer.
5. Spoon into bowls or ice cream glasses with a few watermelon balls on top.

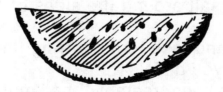

SNOW ICE CREAM

Have you ever tasted homemade ice cream made with snow?

You Need:
- A can of evaporated milk
- ½ cup of sugar
- 1 teaspoon vanilla
- A large amount of freshly fallen snow

You Do:
1. In a large bowl, mix the milk and the sugar until the sugar is dissolved. Then add the vanilla.
2. Stir in the fresh snow. (Add as much snow as you need for the taste and look of vanilla ice cream.)
3. For an added treat, pour a little maple syrup or chocolate sauce over the top.
4. Eat it all up before it melts.!

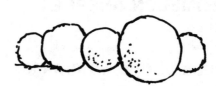

Pack away a few snowballs in your freezer to use from time to time—or to have a **snowball fight** next summer!

VANILLA ICE CREAM

1. Beat together in a 1 lb. coffee can 1 egg and ¼ cup of honey.
2. Add 1 cup milk, ½ cup cream, 1 teaspoon vanilla, ¼ teaspoon salt
3. Cover with the plastic lid.
4. Place the can in an old bucket or pail and a layer of ice (cubes or crushed) on the bottom and sprinkle with rock salt.
5. Pack more ice and salt around the sides of the can—almost to the top.
6. Remove the cover and take turns stirring the ice cream mixture, turning the can as you do it.
7. After 15-30 minutes your cream will be "mushy" enough to eat—**or** if you prefer it to be harder place the can in the freezer for several hours.

ICE CREAM SUNDAES

Did you know that the name for this delicious ice cream concoction came from the word Sunday? Years ago people were not allowed to sip ice cream sodas through a straw on that day, so they made up a **Sunday treat** that could be eaten with a spoon.

PEANUT BUTTER-FUDGE SAUCE

You Need:
- 1 (6 oz.) package of semi-sweet chocolate pieces
- ⅓ cup of milk
- ½ cup of peanut butter
- ¼ cup of corn syrup
- ½ teaspoon vanilla

You Do:
1. Bring all of the ingredients except the vanilla to a boil in a saucepan, stirring constantly.
2. Remove from heat and stir in the vanilla.
3. Serve warm. Yum!

CARAMEL

You Need:
- 1 cup of packed down brown sugar
- ¼ cup of milk
- 2 Tablespoons butter or margarine
- 1 teaspoon vanilla

You Do:
   Same directions as above

COW SHAKES

CHOCOLATE OR CAROB COW DRINK
(makes 1 glassful)
You Need:

- ¾ cup milk
- 2 teaspoons honey
- ¼ cup cocoa or carob powder
- 1 ice cube

You Do:
1. Put in blender and whirl until mixed.
2. Enjoy!

Luscious Lavender Cow
- 1 banana (ripe)
- ¼ cup grape juice
- ½ cup ice cubes
- ¾ cup pineapple juice
- 1 cup buttermilk or yogurt

Blend until smooth.

(makes 2-3 servings)

Pink Elephant
- 1 banana
- 1 cup buttermilk or yogurt
- 3-4 large strawberries
- 3-4 ice cubes
- 1 tablespoon honey (optional)

Blend until smooth.

(makes 1-2 servings)

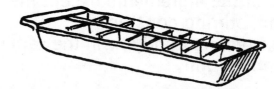

ORANGE SHAKE-EM-UP
(1-2 servings)

You Need:
- 2 heaping teaspoonfuls of orange soft drink mix (powdered)
- 1 cup of cold milk
- Orange ice cubes*

You Do:
1. Add the drink mix to the milk in a glass or shaker.
2. Stir or shake until dissolved.
3. Fill with orange ice cubes.
    * To make orange ice cubes, stir 4 heaping teaspoonfuls of drink mix into 2 cups of milk. Pour into an ice cube tray and freeze.

CHOCOLATE PEPPERMINT MILK SHAKE
(makes two to three servings)

You Need:
- 1 pint vanilla ice cream
- ⅓ cup of chocolate flavor milk-mix
- 2 cups of cold milk
- Dash peppermint extract
- more scoops of Vanilla ice cream
- Crushed peppermint stick candy

You Do:
1. Beat the ice cream and milk-mix with a blender or a mixer until smooth.
2. Add milk, and extract, whip just until foamy.
3. Top each serving with a scoop of ice cream and sprinkle with candy. **Use a spoon and a straw for this yummy drink!**

TIGER TREATS

Add Tiger's milk (a powdered nutrition booster that comes in a variety of flavors) to cold milk. Stir or shake well before serving.

BEDTIME BANANA DRINK

You Need:
- a ripe banana
- 1 cup of milk, ice cream or yogurt
- a peach or nectarine, cut up
- a few strawberries, raspberries or blueberries

You Do:
1. Place everything in your blender and whirl until smooth.
2. If too thick, add a little milk.
   Banana tip: Put left-over or too-ripe bananas in your freezer until ready to use for a drink or dessert.

POPSICLE FUN

LICKING-GOOD FRUIT YOGURT POPS

You Need:
- 1 6 oz. can of frozen orange or grape juice concentrate
- 1 6 oz. can of water
- 1 cup yogurt (plain or fruit-flavored)
- cut-up fresh fruit: berries, bananas, peaches or apricots

You Do:
1. Whirl all of the ingredients including the fruit* in your blender, and pour into small paper cups.
2. Place in freezer until partly frozen, then insert wooden sticks for handles.
3. When firm, peel off the cups and enjoy!
   * The fruit can be diced into tiny pieces and spooned into the cups before filling, if you prefer.

FRUIT POPS

You Need:
- 1 pint of strawberries, hulled (or any kind of fresh fruit)
- 1 cup of plain yogurt, milk or cream
- 2-3 Tablespoons honey, to taste

You Do:
1. Blend all ingredients until smooth (a shorter time if you like chunks of berries).
2. Pour into paper cups or molds and place in freezer.
3. When partially frozen, put a popsicle stick into each one.
4. Wait an hour or two, then peel off the cups and enjoy!

...A Special Treat
PEANUT BUTTER BANANA POPS

You Need:
- ¼ cup chunky peanut butter
- ¼ cup non-fat dry milk
- 1 teaspoon honey
- 1/3 cup light cream
- 4 bananas
- 1/3 cup chopped nuts

You Do:
1. Blend the peanut butter, milk, honey and cream until smooth.
2. Peel the bananas, wrap in plastic or foil and freeze until hard.
3. Dip the frozen bananas into the peanut butter mixture (tongs work well); then roll in nuts...
4. Wrap in plastic or foil and put **back** in the freezer...or eat immediately!

YOGURT POPSICLES

You Need:
- two packages (3 oz.) orange or raspberry gelatin
- two cups boiling water
- 3 Tablespoons honey
- two containers vanilla yogurt **(8 oz)**
- paper cups and popsicle sticks

You Do:
1. Dissolve the gelatin in boiling water; then chill until slightly thickened.
2. Beat the yogurt and honey into the gelatin and blend it until smooth.
3. Pour the mixture into paper cups and freeze for an hour or so; then push in popsicle sticks and return to freezer.

Makes 12 popsicles.

NO-BAKE IDEAS

NO-BAKE COOKIES

You Need:
- 2 cups sugar
- ¼ stick margarine, softened
- ½ cup milk
- ¼ cup cocoa or carob powder
- 1 teaspoon vanilla
- ½ cup peanut butter (optional)
- 3 cups uncooked oatmeal

You Do:
1. Combine the sugar, margarine, milk and cocoa in a pot.
2. Bring to a boil, then let boil for about a minute, stirring carefully.
3. Remove from the heat and add the vanilla, peanut butter and oatmeal.
4. Mix well, then drop by spoonfuls onto waxed paper.
5. Let cool and enjoy!

NO-BAKE GRAHAM CRACKER COOKIES

You Need:
- 1 cup raisins
- 1 cup chopped dates
- ¼ cup honey
- 10 Graham crackers

You Do:
1. Put the raisins, dates, honey and crushed graham crackers into a mixing bowl, mix together with a spoon, fork or your hands.
2. Crush the graham crackers (with a rolling pin, or in a plastic bag with your fingers)
3. Roll into balls.

CHECKERBOARD COOKIES

You Need:
- 1 package miniature marshmallows
- ¼ cup of margarine
- 2 packages semi-sweet chocolate bits
- 1 cup of peanut butter

You Do:
1. Line a brownie pan (9x9) with aluminum foil.
2. Pour the marshmallows on the bottom.
3. Melt the chocolate and margarine, then stir in the peanut butter, and pour the mixture over the marshmallows.
4. Place the pan in the refrigerator until cold. Cut into squares and eat.

NO-BAKE PIE-CRUSTS

Use your imagination for the filling: layers of ice cream (use any combination you like), whipped cream or yogurt and fresh fruits; or a pudding mix topped with Dream Whip and cherries.

OREO™ COOKIE

You Need:
- a small package of Oreo cookies
- 2 tablespoons margarine or butter

You Do:
1. Crush the cookies in a blender or food processor (and watch the white disappear!)
2. Stir in the melted margarine, then press the cookie mixture into a 9" pie tin.

GRAHAM CRACKER

You Need:
- 1¼ cups graham crackers
- ¼ cup sugar or 2 tablespoons honey
- ¼ cup butter or margarine (melted)

You Do:

Follow the Oreo cookie directions, adding the sugar along with the butter. Press into a pie pan.

COOKIES

ICE CREAM COOKIES
   (Makes about 4 dozen)

You Need:
- 1 cup chocolate ice cream
- 1⅛ cups biscuit mix
- ⅛ cup sugar
- ¼ teaspoon cinnamon
- ½ pkg. (3 oz.) semi-sweet chocolate curls or carob chips

You Do:
1. Heat oven to 375 degrees.
2. Put the ice cream into a bowl and let it stand at room temperature for about 5 minutes.
3. Grease a cookie sheet.
4. Stir the biscuit mix, sugar and cinnamon into the ice cream and mix until smooth.
5. Then stir in the chocolate chips.
6. Drop the dough from a teaspoon on the cookie sheet about 3 inches apart. Store remaining in refrigerator while the cookies are baking. Bake in 375 degree oven 8 to 10 minutes (until tops of cookies are dry).

BUTTER COOKIES

You Need:
- 1 cup butter or margarine (2 sticks)
- 2 cups flour
- powdered sugar (optional)
- ¼ cup honey
- 2 tablespoons vanilla
- ¾ cup chopped nuts

You Do:
1. Cream the shortening and honey together.
2. Then add the flour, vanilla and nuts.
3. Shape into ½" balls and flatten slightly with a fork or your palm.
4. Bake on a lightly-greased cookie sheet at 350° for 10-12 minutes.
5. When cool, sprinkle with confectioners' sugar, if you wish. Or spread a lemon frosting on top.

AGGRESSION COOKIES

(Great for "Letting off Steam")

You Need:
- 3 cups of oatmeal
- 1½ cups of whole wheat flour
- 1½ teaspoons of baking powder
- nuts
- 1½ cups of brown sugar
- 1½ cups of margarine or butter
- raisins
- seeds

You Do:
1. Dump all of the ingredients into a large bowl.
2. Using both hands, squish, squash and mash everything together.
3. Keep on kneading the dough as long and as hard as you feel like doing it; then roll bits of dough into balls and place far apart on a cookie sheet.
4. Flatten with you hand or with the bottom of a small glass dipped into sugar and bake at 350 degrees for 10-12 minutes. When cool, eat!!!

GREAT GRANDMA'S SAND TARTS

You Need:
- ½ cup of butter
- 1 cup of sugar
- 2 eggs
- 2 cups of flour
- 1 teaspoon baking soda
- eggwhites
  sugar and cinnamon

You Do:
1. Cream the butter and sugar together; then add the eggs (beaten slightly).
2. Sift the flour and baking powder and slowly stir it into the creamed mixture.
3. Knead the dough until smooth, then roll into 2 balls and leave in refrigerator for several hours.*
4. Roll out the dough on a floured board as thin as you can.
5. Cut into squares with a fluted knife. Brush tops with eggwhites and sprinkle on cinnamon and sugar (or cocoa).
6. Bake in a 350° oven for 12 to 15 minutes.
   *You could freeze part of the dough to bake later, if you wish. Or make several long rolls of dough and cut into thin slices before baking.

GRANDMA BUHAI'S BROWNIES

You Need:
- 2 oz. bitter chocolate
- ½ cup butter (1 stick)
- 1 cup sugar
- 2 eggs
- powdered sugar
- 1 cup of chopped nuts
- ½ cup flour
- ¼ teaspoon baking soda
- 1 teaspoon vanilla

You Do:
1. Melt the chocolate and butter together in a large saucepan over low heat.
2. Remove from stove and add the sugar, stirring well.
3. Then beat the eggs and add them to the pan.
4. Slowly stir in the flour, baking soda, nuts* and vanilla.
5. Pour into a greased and floured brownie pan and bake at 325° for 25 minutes.
6. When cool, cut into squares and sprinkle with powdered sugar.
   *You could put the nuts on the top, rather than in the batter.

NUT RAISIN COOKIES

You Need:
- 1 cup whole wheat flour
- 1 cup honey
- ¼ teaspoon soda
- ¼ teaspoon salt
- 1 egg
- 1 cup raisins
- 1 cup nuts

You Do:
1. Mix all of the dry ingredients, then add the egg and honey.
2. Mix until you get a stiff dough. (If needed, add enough water or fruit juice to make the dough workable.)
3. Spread on a cookie sheet with sides and bake in a moderate oven (325 degrees) 10 to 15 minutes.
4. Cut into squares while hot.

SUNFLOWER COOKIES

You Need:
- 1¾ cups of all-purpose flour
- ¼ teaspoon baking powder
- a pinch of salt
- ½ cup of butter or margarine
- ¾ cup of sugar
- 1 egg
- ¾ teaspoon grated lemon rind
- ½ Tablespoon lemon juice
- chocolate candy wafers
- yellow decorating sugar

You Do:
1. Sift the flour, baking powder and salt onto a piece of waxed paper.
2. Cream the butter and sugar, then beat in the egg, lemon rind and juice until fluffy.
3. Stir in the flour, a little at a time, until the dough is smooth.
4. Cover and put in refrigerator until firm.
5. Pinch off pieces of dough (about 2 tablespoonfuls) and roll into balls. Place them, 3 inches apart, on lightly greased cookie sheets.
6. Flatten each ball down and press a chocolate wafer into the center.
7. Sprinkle the colored sugar on top and bake at 400° for about 8-10 minutes until the dough is light brown.

HOLIDAY CAKES

CHRISTMAS TREE

Cut and put together the cake pieces. Decorate with gum drops and frosting.

VALENTINE HEARTS

Fill the pans to the same level before baking. Decorate for someone special !

CHANUKAH DREIDEL

Assemble and decorate with blue and white frosting.

Handle   Handle

EASTER BUNNY

Cover with white frosting and sprinkle with coconut. Stick in a candy eye and nose.

Body
Ear — Ear
Head   Tail

BIRTHDAY CLOWN

Decorate with gum drops, jellybeans, licorice sticks, etc.

Face
Hat

FOURTH OF JULY

— Firecracker or Drum —

Pour the batter into a well-greased coffee can. Frost, then decorate with mini-marshmallows, candy bits, licorice or peppermint sticks, etc.

258

VALENTINE POPCORN SHAPES

VALENTINE HEARTS

You Need:
About 5 quarts warm popped corn
  (¾ cup unpopped)
• 1 cup *each* sugar & light corn syrup
• 1 tablespoon white vinegar
• 2 tablespoons water

• pinch of salt
• ¼ cup butter or margarine
• 1½ cups dry-roasted peanuts
  (optional)
• 1 teaspoon vanilla
• ½ teaspoon soda

You Do:
1. Spread popped corn in a large, lightly greased roasting pan and place in a 200° oven.
2. Lightly grease a heart-shaped mold or heart-shaped candy box lined with waxed paper, and set aside.
3. In a heavy 2-quart saucepan, combine the sugar, corn syrup, vinegar, water, and salt. Cook over medium-high heat, stirring often, until mixture reaches 230° on a candy thermometer.
4. Stir in the butter and continue cooking until mixture reaches 260° or soft crack stage. Add peanuts, if desired, and return temperature to 260°.
5. Remove from heat and thoroughly blend in the vanilla and soda. Immediately pour over popped corn and stir with a wooden spoon until popcorn is evenly coated.
6. Grease hands with butter or margarine, and, working as quickly as possible, firmly press enough of the popcorn mixture to fill the mold; then turn out onto waxed paper.
7. Repeat until all of the popcorn mixture has been used. If the mixture hardens before it's molded, set it in a warm oven until the mixture holds its shape when pressed together.
8. Cool hearts thoroughly; wrap in clear plastic wrap. You might add a Valentine card or red ribbon. Makes 5 big hearts.

ST. PATRICK'S DAY

MULLIGAN STEW

You Need:
- one cup diced carrots
- ½ cup of sliced potatoes
- ½ cup of sliced up celery
- 1½ cups of water
- ½ cup of fresh or canned string beans
- one half of a 3 oz. package of dry onion soup mix
- chunks of cooked beef (about 1½ cups)
- ½ cup of sliced onion
- 2 T all purpose flour
- ½ cup of peppers (optional)

You Do:
1. Combine the flour and the soup mix in a large frying pan. Add the water and heat to a boil, stirring constantly.
2. Add the vegetables and the beef; cover and cook over low heat for about an hour and one half, or until the vegetables are tender.

IRISH SODA BREAD

You Need:
- 5 cups flour
- 1 tablespoon salt
- 1 to 2 tablespoons of sugar
- 2 cups buttermilk
- 3 tablespoons baking powder
- 1¾ cups seedless raisins
- 1 teaspoon baking soda

You Do:
1. Sift flour, baking powder, salt and sugar into a large mixing bowl.
2. Stir in the raisins.
3. Add the soda to the buttermilk and pour into the dry mixture, stirring until well mixed.
4. Turn out on a floured board and knead, adding more flour if too sticky.
5. Shape into a round loaf and bake for 1 hour at 350°. When cool, remove from the pan and brush with melted butter.

GELATIN EGGS

GELATIN EASTER EGGS

You Need:
- 1 package fruit-flavored gelatin
- 1 package unflavored gelatin
- masking tape
- 1½ cups of cold water
- 6 blown-out egg shells (with a large hole at one end and a small hole at the other)

You Do:
1. Pour the two gelatins into a saucepan and stir in the water.
2. Heat, stirring constantly, until the gelatin is completely dissolved.
3. Put a piece of masking tape over the small hole in each egg to seal it.
4. Pour the warm gelatin into the large hole, using a small funnel or a spoon.
5. Set the gelatin-filled eggs into an egg carton and place in the refrigerator to harden. (about 3 hours).
6. To crack the shells, roll the eggs on a table, then wet your hands and gently peel off the shell.
7. Keep your gelatin Easter eggs in the refrigerator until ready to eat as a snack; or serve on a nest of green lettuce with shredded carrots and/or a mound of cottage cheese.

MOTHER'S DAY TRAY

A SPECIAL BREAKFAST FOR MOTHER'S DAY

Surprise Mom with a festive breakfast served in bed. If you are well organized and plan in advance, you will avoid the last minute Sunday morning rush and Mom will enjoy her breakfast tray twice as much.

The secret is to plan ahead, do your marketing and some of the cooking the day before; then at the last minute, all you need to do is whip up the orange juice, heat the baked eggs and blueberry muffins, and make the coffee.

You Need:
- 1 6-ounce container of frozen orange juice
- 1 tablespoon fresh lemon juice
- 1 orange slice

You Do:
1. Pour the orange juice concentrate into a blender, add 3 cans of water and lemon juice and mix well. (If you don't have a blender, a wire whisk will do the job for you.)
2. For a festive look, place an orange slice on the rim of the glass by cutting a slit halfway through the slice and hooking it over the glass.

BAKED EGGS AND CHEESE (Makes 4 servings)
(can be made the day before and refrigerated)

You Need:
- 8 slices of bacon
- 1½ slices of firm white bread
- ½ cup milk
- ⅓ cup of water
- ¼ pound of Swiss cheese
- 6 large eggs
- pinch of salt
- pepper to taste
- 2 tablespoons butter
- a 3 cup baking dish, buttered

You Do:
1. Preheat the oven to 400° and place the rack in the middle of the oven.
2. Cook the bacon slowly until crisp; drain on paper toweling. When cooked, break 5 slices into pieces and set aside. Save the remaining three slices to use later.
3. Cut the crusts off the bread and break them into small pieces. Place in a dish and add the milk and water.
4. While the bread is soaking in the liquid, shred the cheese and set it aside.
5. Then break the eggs into a bowl and add salt and pepper to taste.
6. Squeeze the liquid out of the breadcrumbs with your hands and add it to the eggs. Beat lightly with an egg beater, fork or whisk.
7. Melt the butter in a skillet and then add the eggs, scrambling them until they are still a little runny.
8. Add the bacon pieces, squeezed out bread and almost all of the grated cheese. Mix until smooth.
9. Place the mixture in the buttered baking dish and sprinkle on the remaining cheese. Arrange the bacon slices in a spoke pattern on top and bake for 15 minutes until lightly browned and bubbly.

Serve your egg and cheese casserole with hot blueberry or corn muffins (made from a mix) and a steaming cup of coffee with a cinnamon stick stirrer.

Happy Mother's (or Father's) Day!

Thanks to Abby Mandel
Glencoe, Illinois, for this idea.

263

HARVEST TREATS

APPLESAUCE "LEATHER" SNACK

1. Heat unsweetened applesauce with some cinnamon in a pan.
2. Place in blender and blend until pureed.
3. Cover a cookie sheet with plastic wrap and spread the sauce out on it (a spatula or egg turner works well).
4. Bake for 8 hours in a 150º oven. Or leave overnight in a low oven with the door ajar.

FRUIT ROLLS (A sweet treat that's good for you!)

You Need: fresh peaches, pears, apples, or nectarines

Quick Method:
You Do:
1. Peel & core fresh peaches, pears, apples or nectarines
2. Blend in a blender until smooth.
3. Cook over moderate heat for 5 mintues. Cool & wrap in plastic. Roll up like a jelly roll.

DRIED FRUIT AND SQUASHES

Sun dried fruits and melon strips were and still are a welcome addition to winter meals and supply vitamins, as well as flavorful fillings for pies and turnovers.

The Pueblo people gather wild plums to dry; and use the peaches, apricots and apples from their orchards, as well as *melons* and *squashes* from their gardens.

You Do:
1. For melons and squashes, shave off the rind with a sharp knife, cut in half and scrape out all pulp and seeds.
2. Hang the halves to dry in the sun for a day. (A cheesecloth covering will protect the fruit from flies.)
3. Or cut spirally in long strips and hang on a line in the sun.
4. Split and remove the stones from peaches, apricots and plums and spread out on a screen in the sun.

QUICK BREADS

PETER PUMPKIN EATER'S BREAD

Metric Pumpkin Bread

You Need:
- 120 ml Whole Eggs (About 2 eggs)
- 360 ml Sugar
- 240 ml Canned Pumpkin
- 120 ml Cooking Oil
- 2 ml Ground Cloves
- 400 ml Flour
- 120 ml Water
- 2 ml Baking Powder
- 5 ml Baking Soda
- 4 ml Salt
- 2 ml Cinnamon

You Do:
1. Break the eggs, measure and beat. Add the sugar and mix well.
2. Blend in the pumpkin, oil and water.
3. Then stir in all the other ingredients.
4. Fill greased and floured pans ½ full. Bake at 180°C. (350°F.) for 1 hour.

BANANA BREAD

You Need:
- 1 large ripe banana
- ¼ cup oil
- 2¼ cups cake flour
- pinch of baking soda
- 1 cup & 2 tablespoons sugar
- 2 eggs
- ¼ cup all purpose flour
- ¼ cup buttermilk

You Do:
1. Stir all of the ingredients until well blended. The mixture will be a little lumpy.
2. Pour into a cake or muffin pan and bake at 450° for 16-18 minutes.

THANKSGIVING

CRANBERRY SAUCE

You Need:
- 2 cups of fresh cranberries
- 1 cup sugar
- 1 cup water

You Do:
1. Combine the sugar and water in a sauce pan and stir until the sugar dissolves.
2. Bring the mixture to a boil then boil for five more minutes.
3. Add the cranberries and cook about five minutes more until the skins pop open.
4. Serve warm or cold.

CRANBERRY PUDDING CAKE

You Need:
- 1 egg
- 1 cup milk
- 1 stick butter
- 1 cup sugar
- 2 cups flour
- 3 tablespoons baking powder
- pinch of salt
- 2 cups fresh cranberries

You Do:
1. Beat egg, milk, butter and sugar.
2. Stir in the dry ingredients and the cranberries and pour into a greased bread pan. Bake at 350° for ½ hour. When cool, slice and pour butter sauce over the top.

Butter Sauce:

- ½ cup melted butter
- 1 tablespoon flour

Stir together and cook until slightly thick.

RECIPES

WHOLE WHEAT MUFFINS

You Need:
- 2 cups whole wheat flour
- 1 tablespoon baking powder
- 3 eggs
- ¼ cup milk

- ¼ cup butter, softened
  or ½ safflower margarine cube
- ¼ cup honey

You Do:
1. Mix together the flour and baking powder; then add the eggs, milk, butter and honey. Stir only until the dry ingredients are moist.
2. Spoon into a greased muffin tin or paper muffin cups, ⅔ full.
3. Bake in a preheated 425° oven for 20 minutes until golden brown.

Makes 1 dozen.

Variations: Add chopped nuts, cut-up fruits, raisins, etc.

BAKED PUMPKIN

You Need:
- 1 small pumpkin, peeled and cubed
- 1 cup sugar
- 1 teaspoon salt
- cinnamon (optional)

You Do:
1. Put the pumpkin cubes in a baking dish and sprinkle with sugar and salt.
2. Cover the pan with foil and bake in a moderate oven until soft.
3. Shake cinnamon over the warm pumpkin.

BETTY'S CORN PUDDING CASSEROLE

You Need:
- 1 can of cream style corn
- 3 eggs
- ¼ cup of milk
- 2 Tablespoons flour
- 2 Tablespoons sugar
- ½ stick of butter

You Do:
1. Mix together 2 tablespoons of corn with the flour and sugar.
2. Add the rest of the corn.
3. Then beat the eggs and add them along with the milk.
4. Melt the butter; use some to grease your casserole. Pour the rest into the corn mixture. Stir well.
5. Bake at 400° for 45 minutes.

CORN DUMPLINGS

You Need:
- 1 cup flour
- 1 teaspoon baking powder
- 3 tablespoons cornmeal
- 1 cup fresh corn from the cob
- (or canned whole kernel corn)
- salt to taste

You Do:
1. Mash the corn thoroughly or grate in a blender.
2. Mix all ingredients until well blended.
3. Add water if necessary, but keep dough fairly stiff.
4. Drop the dumpling mixture by heaping tablespoonfuls into soup or a stew, cover and simmer 8-10 minutes.

CORN ROAST

When roasting fresh ears of corn outdoors, wait until the wood fire has died down to embers and the charcoal in a grill is glowing coals.

Turn the husk back and strip off the silk. Then close the husk up and lay the corn on the embers. Roast for 15-20 minutes, carefully turning a few times. (Use tongs and asbestos mitts.) Strip off the husks and enjoy!

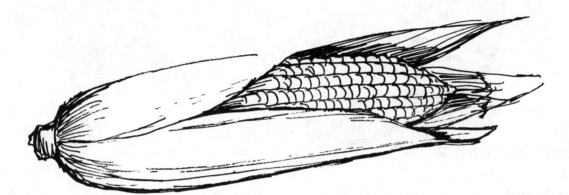

AN INDIAN HYMN OF THANKS TO MOTHER CORN

"See! The Mother Corn comes hither, making all hearts glad!
Making all hearts glad!
Giving her thanks, she brings a blessing; now, behold! she is here!

Yonder Mother Corn is coming, coming unto us!
Coming unto us!
Peace and plenty she is bringing; now, behold!
she is here!"

CHRISTMAS TREATS

GINGERBREAD PEOPLE

You Need:
- ¼ cup shortening
- ½ cup brown sugar
- ⅓ cup cold water
- ¾ cup dark molasses
- ½ teaspoon ginger
- raisins and icing for decoration
- 3 cups of flour
- 1 teaspoon baking soda
- ½ teaspoon salt
- ½ teaspoon allspice
- ½ teaspoon cinnamon

You Do:
1. Mix together the shortening, sugar, water and molasses.
2. Then add the flour, soda, and spices, stirring gently.
3. Mix well with a spoon and knead with your hands.
4. Wrap in wax paper and chill in the refrigerator until quite cold.
5. Roll **small balls** of the dough for heads and bodies, and arrange them on a piece of aluminum foil. Roll some snakes for arms and legs, and attach these to the balls. Overlap the dough pieces and flatten them down.
6. Push in **raisins** for eyes, noses, mouths and buttons.
7. Bake your **people cookies** for 10 to 15 minutes in a 375⁰ oven.
8. When cool, frost with icing, if you wish.
   You could also roll out the dough and use cookie-cutters to make your gingerbread people.

CHRISTMAS GUMDROP CAKE

You Need:
- a box of cake mix (white or yellow)
- ½ cup orange juice
- 2 tablespoons grated orange peel
- 2½ cups (a 16 oz. package of small gumdrops)
- 1 cup walnuts
- 1 tablespoon grated lemon peel

You Do:
1. Mix the cake mixture together according to the directions on the package.
2. Add the cinnamon, nutmeg and orange juice.
3. Mix in the gumdrops, walnuts, grated orange and lemon peel. Spread the batter in a greased and floured 12 inch tube pan.
4. Bake in a 300° oven according to the directions on the cake mix.
5. Immediately remove from the pan and cool on a wire rack.
6. Frost with your favorite flavor of frosting then decorate with candy sprinkles, red and green sugar, cut-up gum drops, etc.

GINGERBREAD HORN BOOKS
(a special treat on Christmas morning)

1. Follow the same gingerbread recipe as you did for the cookies [or use a mix].
2. Roll out the dough and cut it in the shape of an old fashioned **horn book** (a wooden **paddle** to which writing paper was attached).
3. Write letters of the alphabet, numbers or your name on it with a pointed dowel, toothpick or your finger.
4. Bake, and let cool; then frost.

Legend tells us that parents and teachers sometimes left this note tied to the gaily wrapped horn book cookie, "knowledge is hereby devoured by ye childe and a glad yeare with great wealth of learning becomes in store."

BIBLIOGRAPHY

For Parents and Teachers

Abraham, Willard. *Living with Preschoolers.* Tuscon, Arizona: O'Sullivan, Woodside & Co., 1976.

Beadle, Muriel. *A Child's Mind.* Garden City, New York: Doubleday & Co., 1970.

Caldwell, Betty, *et al. Home Teaching Activities.* Little Rock, Arkansas: Center for Early Development in Education, 1972.

Caplan, Frank and Theresa. *The Power of Play.* Garden City, New York: Doubleday & Co., 1973.

Carfield, Jack and Wells, H.C. *100 Ways to Enhance Self-Concept in the Classroom.* Englewood Cliffs, New York: Prentice-Hall, 1976.

Dodson, Fitzhugh. *How to Parent.* New York: Signet Books, 1971.

Elkind, David. *A Sympathetic Understanding of the Child.* Boston: Allyn and Bacon, 1974.

Fleming, Bonnie and Hamilton, Darlene. *Resources for Creative Teaching.* New York: Harcourt Brace, 1977.

Fraiberg, Selma H. *The Magic Years.* New York: Scribner Library, 1959.

Garfield, Nancy and Richardson, Lynn J. *Education for Parenthood Child Development Guide.* New York: Girl Scouts of America, 1974.

Hartley, R. and Goldenson, R. *The Complete Book of Children's Play.* New York: T. Crowell Co., 1963.

Hymes, James L. Jr. *Effective Home-School Relations.* Los Angeles: Southern Association for the Education of Young Children, 1971.

_____ . *Teaching the Child Under Six.* Los Angeles: Southern Association for the Education of Young Children.

_____ .*Three to Six: Your Child Starts to School.* Public Affairs Pamphlet *ff/*163, 1978.

Isaacs, Susan. *The Children We Teach: Seven to Eleven Years.* New York: Schocken Books, 1971.

Kaplan, Kaplan, Madsen, Gould. *A Young Child Experiences.* Santa Monica: Goodyear, 1975.

Kelly and Parsons, *Mother's Almanac.* New York: Doubleday & Co., 1975.

Larrick, Nancy. *A Parent's Guide to Children's Reading.* New York: Bantam Books, 1975.

Prudden, Bonnie. *How to Keep Your Child Fit from Birth to Six.* New York: Harper and Row, 1964.

Scharlatt, Elizabeth. *Kids Day In, Day Out.* New York: Simon & Schuster, 1979.

Strom, Robert. *Growing Together: Parent and Child Development.* Monterey, California: Brooks/Dole Publishing, 1978.

Sutton-Smith, Brian and Shirley. *How to Play with Your Children (And When Not To).* New York: Hawthorne Books, Inc., 1974.

General Activities

Barrata-Lorton, Mary. *Workjobs for Parents.* Menlo Park, California: Addison-Wesley, 1975.

_____ . *Workjobs for Parents II.* Menlo Park, California: Addison-Wesley, 1979.

Blake, Jim and Ernst, Barbara. *The Great Perpetual Learning Machine.* Boston: Little, Brown and Co., 1976.

Boston Children's Medical Center. *What to Do When There's Nothing to Do.* New York: Dell, 1967.

Broad & Butterworth. *The Playgroup Handbook.* New York: St. Martin's Press, 1974.

Burton, Leon and Hughes, William. *Music Play.* Menlo Park, California: Addison-Wesley, 1979.

Caney, Steve. *Steve Caney's Play Book.* New York: Workman Publishing Co., 1975.

_____. *Steve Caney's Toy Book.* New York: Workman Publishing Co., 1972.

_____. *Kids America.* New York: Workman Publishing Co., 1978.

Cardozo, Peter. *The Whole Kids Catalog.* New York: Bantam Books, 1975.

_____. *The 2nd Whole Kids Catalog.* New York: Bantam Books, 1978.

Carmichael, Viola. *Curriculum Ideas for Young Children.* Los Angeles: Southern Association for the Education of Young Children, 1971.

Cherry, Clare. *Creative Play for the Developing Child.* Belmont, California: Fearon-Pitman, 1976.

_____. *Creative Movement for the Developing Child.* Belmont, California: Fearon-Pitman, 1971.

Cole, Haas, Heller, Weinberger. *Children Are Children Are Children.* Boston: Little, Brown and Co., 1978.

Cole, Haas, Bushnell, and Weinberger. *I Saw A Purple Cow and 100 Other Recipes for Learning.* Boston: Little, Brown and Co., 1972.

Colvin, Mary. *Instructor's Big Idea Book.* Danville, New York: Instructor Publications, Inc., 1978.

Crippled Children's Nursery School Association. *What Can I Do Now Mommy.* Kansas City, Missouri.

Croft and Hess. *An Activities Handbook for Teachers of Young Children.* New York: Houghton Mifflin Co., 1972.

Croft, Doreen. *Recipes for Busy Little Hands.* San Francisco: R. & E. Associates, 1973.

Donahue, Parnell, M.D., and Capellaro, Helen. *Germs Make Me Sick.* New York: Alfred A. Knopf, 1975.

Fiarotta, Phyllis and Fiarotta, Noel. *Be What You Want to Be.* New York: Workman Publishing, 1977.

_____. *Snips and Snales and Walnut Whales.* New York: Workman Publishing Co., 1975.

Gregg, Elizabeth. *What to Do When There's Nothing to Do.* New York: Delacorte Press, 1968.

Hamilton, Alicita, Ed. *Colorado Gold.* Boulder, Colorado: CAEYC, 1977.

Hartman, Harriet. *Let's Play and Learn.* New York: Human Sciences Press, 1976.

Hein, Lucile. *Entertaining Your Child.* New York: Harper and Row, 1971.

Jones, Sandy. *Learning for Little Kids.* Boston: Houghton Mifflin Co., 1979.

Jameson, Kenneth and Kidd, Pat. *Pre-School Play.* New York: Van Nostrand Reinhold, 1974.

Marzollo, Jean and Lloyd, Janice. *Learning through Play.* New York: Harper and Row, 1972.

McCoy, Elin. *Year-Round Playbook.* New York: Random House, 1979.

McElderry, Joanne and Escobedo, Linda. *Tools for Learning.* Denver: Love Publishing Co. 1979.

Mercer Island Preschool Association. *Rainy Day Activities for Preschoolers.* Alderwood Manor, Washington: Warren Publishing.

Paxmon, Shirley and Monroe. *To Bed To Bed the Doctor Said.* Walnut Creek, California: Evergreen Press, 1975.

Price, Shirley S. and Merle E. *The Primary Math Lab.* Santa Monica, California: Goodyear, 1978.

Rich, Dorothy. *Success for Children!* Washington, D.C.: The Home and School Institute, 1972.

Rice, Mary F. and Flatter, Charles F. *Help Me Learn.* Englewood Cliffs, New Jersey: Prentice Hall.

Rudolph, Marguerita. *From Hand to Head.* New York: McGraw Hill, 1973.

Stranks, Susan. *Family Fun.* Woodbury, New York: Barron's Educational Series, Inc.

Vance, Eleanor. *The Everything Book.* New York: Western Publishing, 1974.

Winn, Marie and Porcher, Mary Ann. *The Playgroup Book.* New York: Macmillan, 1967.

Zubrowski, Bernie. Children's Museum Activity Books, *Ball Point Pens; Bubbles; Milk Carton Blocks.* Boston: Little, Brown, 1979.

Arts & Crafts

Cherry, Clare. *Creative Art for the Developing Child.* Belmont, California: Fearon-Pitman, 1972.

Fiarotta, Phyllis. . *Nostalgia Crafts Book.* New York: Workman Publishing, 1975.

Hoople, Cheryl G. *The Heritage Sampler.* N.Y.: Dial Press, 1975.

Kinser, Charleen. *Outdoor Art for Kids.* Chicago: Follett Publishing, 1975.

LeFevre, Gregg. *Junk Sculpture.* New York: Sterling Publishing Co., 1973.

Linderman, C. Emma. *Teachables from Trashables.* St. Paul: Toys 'N Things, 1979.

Newsome, A.J. *Crafts and Toys from around the World.* New York: Simon and Schuster, 1972.

Parker, Xenia Ley. *A Beginner's Book of Off-Loom Weaving.* New York: Dodd, Mead, 1978.

Romberg, Jenean. *Arts and Crafts Discovery Units.* New York: The Center for Applied Research in Education, 1975.

Sattler, Helen. *Recipes for Art and Craft Materials.* New York: Lothrop, Lee & Shepard, 1973.

Schnacke, Dick. *American Folk Toys: How to Make Them.* Baltimore: Penguin Books, Inc. 1974.

Vermeer and Larivierd. *The Little Kid's Craft Book.* New York: Taplinger Publishing Co., 1975.

Weiss, Harvey. *Beginning Artist's Library.* Reading, Massachusetts: Addison-Wesley, 1978.

Wiseman, A. *Making Things, The Book of Creative Discovery.* Boston: Little, Brown, Book I, 1975.

Wiseman, A. *Making Things, The Book of Creative Discovery.* Boston: Little, Brown, Book II, 1976.

Yerian, Cameron and Yerian, Margaret. *Funtime Handmade Toys and Games.* Chicago: Children's Press, 1975.

Science and Nature

Abruscato, Joe and Hassard, Jack. *The Whole Cosmos Catalogue of Science Activities for Kids.* Santa Monica, California: Goodyear, 1978.

Aileen, Paul. *Kids' Outdoor Gardening.* New York: Doubleday & Co., 1978.

Allen, Janet. *Exciting Things To Do with Nature Materials.* Philadelphia: J.B. Lippincott Co., 1977.

Allison, Linda. *The Reason for Seasons.* Boston: Little, Brown & Co., 1975.

_____ . *Sierra Club Summer Book.* New York: Charles Scribner's Sons, 1977.

_____ . *The Wild Inside.* New York: Charles Scribner's Sons, 1979.

Bowden, A.O. *Wild Green Things in the City.* New York: T.Y. Crowell & Co., 1972.

Caras, Roger. *A Zoo in Your Room.* New York: Harcourt Brace Janovich, 1975.

Chinery, M. *Enjoying Nature with Your Family.* New York: Crown Publishing, 1977.

Clark, Collins and Collins. *The Naturalist/Nature Walk.* Provo, Utah: Press Publishing, 1972.

_____ . *The Naturalist/Botanical Art.* Provo, Utah: Press Publishing, 1972.

Cobb, Vicki. *Science Experiments You Can Eat.* New York: Lippincott, 1973.

DeVito, Alfred and Krockover, Gerald. *Creative Sciencing.* Boston: Little, Brown & Co., 1976.

Eckstein and Gleit. *Fun with Growing Things.* New York: Avon Books, 1975.

Garelick, May. *It's About Birds.* New York: Holt, Rinehart & Winston, 1978.

Gray, William R. *Camping Adventure.* National Geographic Society, 1976.

Hillcourt, William. *The Official Boy Scout Handbook.* 9th Ed., 1979.

Hussey and Pacino. *Collecting for the City Naturalists.* New York: T.Y. Crowell, 1972.

Inger. Eve. *Weather on the Move.* Reading, Massachusetts: Addison Wesley, 1970.

Langford, Michael. *Starting Photography.* New York: Hastings House, 1976.

Peterson, Roger T. *Field Guide to the Birds.* San Francisco: Houghton Mifflin Books, 1968.

Petrich and Dalton. *The Kids' Garden Book.* Concord, California: Nitty Gritty Productions, 1974.

Renner, A.G. *How to Build A Better Mousetrap Car and Other Experimental Fun.* N.Y.: Dodd, Mead, 1977.

Schaeffer, Elizabeth. *Dandelion, Pokeweed and Goosefoot.* Reading, Massachusetts: Addison-Wesley, 1978.

Selsam and Hunt. *A First Look at the World of Plants.* New York: Walker & Co., 1978.

Shapiro, Irwin. *Smokey Bear's Camping.* New York: Golden Press, 1976.

Simons, Robin. *Recyclopedia.* Boston: Houghton Mifflin Co., 1976.

Skelsey and Huckaby. *Growing Up Green.* New York: Workman Publishing, 1973.

Surcouf, Lorraine. *Growing a Green Thumb.* New York: Barron's Educational Series, Inc., 1975.

Games

Bentley, W.J. *Indoor and Outdoor Games.* Belmont, California: Fearon Publishers, 1966.

Ferretti, F. *The Great American Book of Sidewalk, Stoop, Dirt, Curb, and Alley Games.* New York: Workman Publishing Co., 1975.

Frankel, Lillian and Godfrey. *101 Best Nature Games and Projects.* New York: Gramercy Publishing Co., 1959.

Gallagher, Rachel. *Games in the Street.* New York: Four Winds Press, 1977.

Hall, Sweeny and Esser. *Until the Whistle Blows.* Santa Monica, California: Goodyear Publishing, 1977.

Hockerman, Dennis. *Sidewalk Games.* Milwaukee: Raintree Children's Books, 1978.

Langstaff and Langstaff. *Shimmy Shimmy Coke-Ca-Pop.* New York: Doubleday and Co., 1973.

McLenighan, Valjean. *International Games.* Milwaukee: Raintree Children's Books, 1978.

Michaelis, Bill and Dolores. *Learning Through Noncompetitive Activities and Play.* Maple Plain, Minnesota: Learning Handbooks, 1979.

Nelson, Esther L. *Movement Games for Children of All Ages.* New York: Sterling Publishing Co., 1975.

O'Quinn, Garland, Jr. *Developmental Gymnastics.* Austin, Texas: U. of Texas Press, 1977.

Orlick, Terry. *The Cooperative Sports and Games Book.* New York: Pantheon, 1978.

Resnick, Michel. *Gymnastics and You.* Chicago: Rand McNally, 1977.

Skolnik, Peter. *Jump Rope!* New York: Workman Publishing Co., 1974.

Tatlow, Peter. *Gymnastics.* New York: Atheneum, 1978.

Wagner, Gilloley and Roth, Cesinger. *Games and Activities for Early Childhood Education.* Darien, Connecticut: Teachers Publishing Corp., 1967.

Werner, Peter H. *A Movement Approach to Games for Children.* St. Louis: C.V. Mosby Co., 1979.

Rhymes, Fingerplays and Poems

Beall, Pam and Nipp, Susan. *Wee Sing.* Alderwood Manor, Washington: Warren Publishing, 1975.

Cromwell, Liz and Hibner, Dixie. *Finger Frolics.* Partner Press, 1977.

Flint Public Library. *Ring A Ring O'Roses.* Flint Board of Education, 1971.

Glazer, Tom. *Eye Winker Tom Tinker Chin Chopper.* Garden City, New York: Doubleday & Co., 1973.

Infantino, Cynthia, Ed. *Going on A Finger Play Hunt.* Wheeling, Illinois: CLU/RLAC, 1977.

Jenkins, Ella. *Ella Jenkins Songbook.* Chicago.

Matterson, Elizabeth. *This Little Puffin.* Middlesex, England: Penguin Books, 1972.

McCord, David. *One At A Time.* Boston: Little, Brown and Co., 1977.

Silverstein, Shel. *Where the Sidewalk Ends.* New York: Harper and Row, 1974.

Thompson. *All the Silver Pennies.* New York: Macmillan, 1967.

Wailes and Westerberg. *Fingerplays, Rhymes and Riddles.* Libertyville, Illinois: Media Workshop, 1974.

Zeitlin, Patty. *Castle in My City.* Sierra Madre, California: SCAEYC. 1968

Holidays

Barth, Edna. *Holly, Reindeer and Colored Lights.* New York: Seabury Press, 1971.

_____ .*Lilies, Rabbits and Painted Eggs.* New York: Seabury Press, 1970.

Becker, Joyce. *Jewish Holiday Crafts.* New York: Bonim Books, 1977.

Cole, Haas, Heller, Weinberger. *A Pumpkin in a Pear Tree.* Boston: Little, Brown and Co., 1976.

Cram, Dorothy, E. *Games for Special Days.* Dansville, N.Y.: Instructor Publications, Inc., 1963.

Creekmoore, Betsey. *Making Gifts from Oddments and Outdoor Materials.* New York: Hearthside, 1970.

Educational Insights, Inc. (ed.). *Creative Holidays.* Inglewood, Calif., 1971.

Fiarotta, Phyllis. *Confetti.* New York: Workman Publishing, 1978.

Forte, Pangel and Tupa. *Pumpkins, Pinwheels and Peppermint Packages.* Incentive Publications, 1974.

Harelson, Randy. *Amazing Days.* New York: Workman Publishing, 1979.

Kohl, Marguerite and Young, Frederica. *The Holiday Book.* New York: David McKay and Co., 1952.

Mannings-Sanders, Ruth *Festivals.* E.P. Dutton & Co., 1972.

Newmann, Dara. *The Teacher's Almanac.* New York: Center for Applied Research, 1973.

Robbins, Ireene. *Elementary Teacher's Arts and Crafts Ideas for Every Month of the Year.* W. Nyack, N.Y.: Parker Publishing Co., 1970.

Temko, Florence. *Folk Crafts for World Friendship.* New York: Doubleday, 1976.

Wilt, Joy and Watson, Terre. *Seasonal and Holiday Happenings.* Waco, Texas: Creative Resources, 1978.

Carpentry

Adkins, H. *Toolchest: A Primer of Woodcraft.* New York: Walker and Co., 1973.

Bubel and Bubel. *Working Wood. A Guide for the Country Carpenter.* Emmaus, Pennsylvania: Rodale Press, 1977.

DeCristoforo, R.J. *Handtool Handbook for Woodworking.* Tucson, Arizona: HP Books, 1977.

McPhee Gribble Publishers, Ed. *Carpentry.* Australia: Penguin Books, 1976.

Newman, T.T. *Woodcraft: Basic Concepts and Skills.* Radnor, Pennsylvania: Chilton Book Co., 1976.

Patrick. *Tools for Woodworking,* Drake Homecraftsman Series, New York: Drake Publishers, 1976.

Peterson, Franklyn. *Children's Toys You Can Build Yourself.* Englewood Cliffs, New Jersey: Prentice Hall, 1978.

Pettit, Florence. *Whirligigs and Whimmy Diddles.* New York: T.Y. Crowell Co., 1972.

Simmons, John. *Carpentry Is Easy — When You Know How.* New York: Arco Publishing.

Tangerman, E.J. *1001 Designs for Whittling and Wood Carving.* New York: McGraw Hill, 1976.

Torre. Frank. *Woodworking for Kids.* New York: Doubleday, 1978.

Cooking

Abisch and Kaplan. *The Munchy, Crunchy Healthy Kid's Snack Book.* New York: Walker & Co., 1976.

Amana Refrigeration Inc. Home Economics Staff, *Crunchies, Munchies and Hamburgers Too.* Radarange Microwave Oven Recipes, Amana, Iowa, 1978.

Ault, Roz and Uranek, Liz. *Kids Are Natural Cooks.* Boston: Houghton Mifflin Co., 1974.

Bruna and Dakan. *Cooking in the Classroom.* Belmont, California: Fearon Publishers, 1975.

Burns, Marilyn. *Good for Me!* Boston: Little, Brown and Co., 1978.

Cadwallader and Ohr. *The Whole Earth Cook Book.* New York: Bantam Books, 1972.

_____ . *Cooking Adventures for Kids.* San Francisco: Houghton Mifflin Books, 1974.

Cavin, Ruth. *1 Pinch of Sunshine, = Cup of Rain.* New York: Atheneum, 1975.

Cobb, Vicki. *Arts and Crafts You Can Eat.* New York: Lippincott Co., 1974.

Cooper, Jane. *Love at First Bite.* New York: Alfred A. Knopf, 1977.

Croft, Karen. *The Good for Me Cookbook,* San Francisco: R. & E. Associates, 1971.

Cross and Fiske. *Backpacker's Cookbook.* Berkeley, California: Ten Speed Press, 1974.

Edge, Nellie. *Kindergarten Cooks.* Port Angeles, Washington: Pen Print, 1975.

Feingold, Dr. Ben. *The Feingold Cookbook for Hyperactive Children.* New York: Random House, 1979.

Ferriera, Nancy. *Mother-Child Cookbook.* Menlo Park, California: Pacific Coast, 1970.

Friedman. *I Ate the Whole Thing Cookbook.*

Glovach, Linda. *Potions, Lotions, Tonics and Teas.* Englewood Cliffs, New Jersey: Prentice-Hall, 1977.

_____ . *The Little Witch's Black Magic Cookbook.* Englewood Cliffs, New Jersey: Prentice Hall, 1972.

Goodwin, Mary T. and Pollen, Gerry. *Creative Food Experiences for Children.* Washington, D.C.: Center for Science in the Public Interest, 1974.

Harms and Veitch. *Cook and Learn: A Child's First Cookbook.* 655 Terra California Drive #3, Walnut Creek, California, 1979.

Johnson, Georgia and Povey, Gail. *Metric Milk Shakes and Witches' Cakes,* New York: Citation Press, 1976.

Lansky, Vicki. *Feed Me I'm Yours.* Wayzata, Minnesota: Meadowbrook Press, 1974.

_____ . *The Taming of the C.A.N.D.Y. Monster.* Wayzata, Minnesota: Meadowbrook Press, 1978.

Lewis, Gail and Shaw, Joan. *Recipes for Learning.* Santa Monica, California: Goodyear Publishing Co., Inc., 1979.

Margoliou, Sidney. *Health Foods: Facts and Fakes.* Public Affairs Pamphlet 498, 1978.

McClellahan and Jaqua. *Cool Cooking for Kids.* Belmont, California: Fearon Publishers, 1976.

Minard, Susan and Berka, Paula. *Eat Alone With Your Children and Like It: A Cooking Manual For Single Parents.* Portola Valley, California: Mynabird Publishing, 1976.

Paul, Aileen. *Kids Camping.* New York: Doubleday and Co., 1973.

Paul and Hawkins. *Kids' Cookbook.* New York: Doubleday and Co., 1975.

Petrich, Dalton. *The Kid's Cookbook.* Concord, California: Nitty Gritty Productions, 1973.

Pizzo, Albert. *Doc Pizzo's Nutrition Handbook.* Newport Beach, California, 1978.

Rogers and Larson. *Let's Do Some Cooking.* Champaign, Illinois: Continuing Education Publications Co., 1977.

Stangl, Jean. *The No-Cook Cookery Cookbook.* Camarillo, Delaware:

Stein, Sara Bonnet, *The Kids' Kitchen Takeover.* New York: Workman Publishing Co., 1975.

Thomas, Dian. *Roughing It Easy I & II.* Provo, Utah: BYU Press, 1974/75.

Walker, Barbara. *The Little House Cook Book.* New York: Harper Junior Books, 1979.

Warren, Jean, Ed. *Seasonal Snack Ideas.* Alder Manor, Washington: Warren Publishing, 1976.

Westover, Eliason. *Make-A-Mix Cookery.* Tucson: H.P. Books.

Wilms, Barbara. *Crunchy Bananas & Other Great Recipes Kids Can Cook.* California: Sagamore Books, 1975.

RESOURCES

AGENCIES

Action for Children's Television, Inc. (ACT)
46 Austin Street
Newtonville, MA 02160

Administration for Children, Youth and Families (ACYF)
U.S. Dept. of Health and Human Services
Washington, DC 20201

American Assoc. of Ed.-Kind.-Nursery Educators (NEA)
1201 16th St., N.W.
Washington, DC 20036

American Home Economics Association
2010 Mass. Ave., N.W.
Washington, DC 20036

American Library Association (ALA)
50 E. Huron Street
Chicago, IL 60611

American Montessori Society
150 Fifth Avenue
New York, NY 10011

Assoc. for Childhood Education Internat'l (ACEI)
3615 Wisconsin Avenue, N.W.
Washington, DC 20016

Assoc. for Children with Learning Disabilities (ACLD)
4156 Library Rd.
Pittsburgh, PA 15234

Black Child Development Institute, Inc.
1463 Rhode Island Avenue, N.W.
Washington, DC 20005

Bureau for the Educationally Handicapped (BEH)
7th and D Streets, S.W.
Office of Education
Washington, DC 20202

Center for the Study of Parent Involvement (CSPI)
5240 Boyd
Oakland, CA 94618

Child Study Association of America
9 East 89th Street
New York, NY 10028

Child Welfare League of America (CWL)
67 Irving Place
New York, NY 10003

Children's Defense Fund
1520 New Hampshire Ave., N.W.
Washington, DC 20036

Council for Exceptional Children (CEC)
1920 Assoc. Dr.
Reston, VA 22091

Day Care Council of America, Inc.
711 14th St., N.W.
Washington, DC 20005

Education Commission of the States
1860 Lincoln, Suite 300
Denver, CO 80295

Family Resource Coalition
230 N. Michigan
Chicago, IL 60601

Family Service Association of America
44 East 23rd Street
New York, NY 10010

Home and School Institute, Inc.
Trinity College
Washington, DC 20017

Institute for Dev. of Home-School Programs
Merrimack Education Center
101 Mill Road
Chelmsford, MA 91824

National Academy of Pediatricians
P.O. Box 1034
Evanston, IL 60204

Nat'l Assoc. for Child Dev. and Education
1800 M Street, N.W.
Washington, DC 20036

Nat'l Assoc. for the Education of Young Children (NAEYC)
1834 Connecticut Avenue, N.W.
Washington, DC 20009

Nat'l Assoc. for Gifted Children
217 Gregory Dr.
Hot Springs, AR 71901

Nat'l Assoc. of the Physically Handicapped
76 Elm Street
London, OH 43140

Nat'l Center for Voluntary Action
1783 Massachusetts Avenue, N.W.
Washington, DC 20036

Nat'l Committee for the Day Care of Children
114 East 32nd Street
New York, NY 10016

Nat'l Consortium for Children and Families
5 Westmoreland Place
Pasadena, CA 91103

Nat'l Education Association
1201 16th St., N.W.
Washington, DC 20036

Nat'l Parents and Teachers Association (PTA)
700 N. Rush Street
Chicago, IL 60611

Nat'l School Volunteer Program, Inc.
300 North Washington Street
Alexandria, VA 22314

Reading is Fundamental
475-L Enfant (Suite 4800)
Washington, DC 20560

Right to Read Program
Office of Education
400 Maryland Ave., Rm. 2128
Washington, DC 20202